HEROES AND LEGENDS

DRAGONSLAYERS

BY JOSEPH A. McCULLOUGH
ILLUSTRATED BY PETER DENNIS

ROSEN
PUBLISHING

NEW YORK

Published in 2015 by The Rosen Publishing Group, Inc.
29 East 21st Street, New York, NY 10010

First Edition

Library of Congress Cataloging-in-Publication Data

McCullough, Joseph A.
Dragonslayers/Joseph A. McCullough.
    pages cm. — (Heroes and legends)
Includes bibliographical references and index.
ISBN 978-1-4777-8136-4 (library bound)
1. Dragons—Juvenile literature. 2. Dragons—Folklore—Juvenile literature. I. Title.
GR830.D7M389 2015
398.24'54—dc23

2014020512

Manufactured in the United States of America

CONTENTS

INTRODUCTION

This is a book of battles, of desperate fights between the greatest heroes of myth and legend and mankind's most ancient and dangerous foe, the dragons. These titanic serpents, with or without wings, or indeed, legs, have haunted the dreams of humanity since our earliest days. In our oldest myths, the gods themselves battled these monsters in an effort to bring order out of chaos, and light out of darkness. In Ancient Babylonian tales, the god Marduk fights against Tiamat, the dragon of chaos. According to the Ancient Greeks, the god Zeus struggled against Typhon, the 'Father of all Monsters', while the sun god Apollo slew the great dragon Python. This last tale is perhaps a reflection of the Ancient Egyptian story where the sun god Ra battles the god of chaos and darkness, Apep, usually depicted as a great serpent or dragon. According to the myths of the Ancient Norse, the struggle against the dragons will continue until the end of time, when Thor will slay Jörmungandr, the Midgard Serpent, as part of Ragnarök, before dying himself from the effects of the serpent's poison.

It is those great battles in the heavens that serve as the backdrop for the stories presented here. This is a book about heroes: men who, despite their mortality, faced off against the dragons and used their strength, skill, and cunning to overcome their enemies. Today, there are literally hundreds of myths, legends, and folktales about dragonslayers. Some of these come from historical, or semi-historical sources; others survive as mere fairytales. To collect them all would be the work of more than one lifetime.

Presented here are the most famous, important, interesting and entertaining stories about dragonslaying. Each tale is retold using modern language and modern storytelling sensibilities, but attempts to stay as true as possible to the original source material. Accompanying each tale is the essential information about the myth or legend: its sources, its historical basis, its development, and its continuing legacy in the modern world.

The story of the dragonslayer is usually considered a European one. It begins in the myths mentioned above and has its strongest roots in the Classical Greek and Ancient Norse stories. These were then filtered through the rise of Christianity, until stories of dragonslayers became part of the make-up of medieval European culture. Although there are dragonslaying stories from other parts of the world, and these will be touched upon in the last chapter of the book, the vast majority of stories, and the enduring legacy of the fight between men and dragons, comes from the European tradition.

Today, thanks in no small part to the writings of J.R.R. Tolkien and the early role-playing game, *Dungeons & Dragons*, dragonslayers have once again become a staple part of modern storytelling and appear in books, comics, and movies too numerous to mention. But there were times, in centuries past, when people truly believed in dragons, when deadly giant serpents with poison breath could lurk in any hole or cave. Those were the days of the great heroes. Those were the days of the dragonslayers.

ANCIENT DRAGONSLAYERS

Many of the early stories of men battling against dragons come from the heroic tales of mythic Greece. In fact, the word "dragon" derives from the Greek word "drakon," meaning "a creature with scales," usually a "serpent or sea-monster." Unfortunately, this immediately leads to a problem. When the Ancient Greeks used the word "drakon" they were not always referring to a creature that modern readers would recognize as a dragon. They could have meant a simple snake or even a shark-like sea-creature. For example, the ancient hero Perseus is sometimes said to have used the head of Medusa to rescue the princess Andromeda from a dragon. However, this is a misreading of "drakon," for the creature described is truly a sea-monster and has no specific dragon-like qualities beyond having scales.

Despite this confusion, the tales of Ancient Greece are full of dragons in the form of giant serpents, often possessing multiple heads and breathing poisonous fumes. Unlike later myths, where dragons seem to have become a true species, almost all of the Greek examples are unique creatures, the offspring of gods, Titans or other monsters. Also, unlike later dragons, these giant serpents are not specifically evil. They are dangerous and usually no friend of mankind, but they embody no specific malice.

While many of the ancient dragonslayer stories in Western culture come from Ancient Greece, there are a few tales of heroes taking on dragons or serpents in other cultures, most notably Celtic and Hebrew, though most of these encounters are just diversions from other adventures, or side-quests from the main story.

Presented below are three of the best known, and most fully elaborated, stories of ancient dragonslayers. Two, the tales of Cadmus and Hercules, come from Ancient Greece, while the third, Daniel of the Lion's Den fame, can be found in the Old Testament of some bibles.

Cadmus, Founder of Thebes

Long before the fall of Troy, the ill-fated King Agenor, son of the sea-god Poseidon, sat on the Phoenician throne and ruled his people with wisdom and justice. The king had three sons, Cadmus, Phoenix, and Cilix and a daughter, Europa, and for many years they lived happily. However, as Europa grew to womanhood, her radiant beauty grew so nearly divine that Zeus himself

came down from Olympus and bore her away. When King Agenor learned of his daughter's disappearance, his grief overwhelmed him. In his madness, he commanded his three sons to go out and search for their sister and not to return unless they found her.

Despite his father's unkind order, Prince Cadmus gathered together a group of companions and set off on this quest. For months he led his men through many adventures, through battles and hardships, but not one clue did they find concerning the missing Europa. In desperation, Cadmus took his men to Delphi in Greece, to consult with the famed Oracle of Apollo. There, where Apollo had slain the dragon, Python, the Oracle instructed Cadmus to abandon his quest, for he would never find his sister. Instead, he should go forth and follow the first animal he encountered until it laid down to rest. In that spot he should found a city.

Troubled by the failure of his quest, Cadmus left the Oracle and returned to his companions. Soon after, he spotted a lone cow, with the sign of the moon on one flank, and decided to follow the beast. For days, Cadmus trudged along after the heifer, which never stopped and never rested, until, finally,

Cadmus Slays the Dragon by Hendrick Goltzius.

Cadmus About to Attack a Dragon by Hendrik Goltzius. (The Bridgeman Art Library)

it settled down in Boeotia. The men rejoiced that they had reached the end of their travels, and Cadmus determined to make a sacrifice to the goddess Athena in thanks. Spying a nearby spring, Cadmus sent his companions off to fetch water, while he prepared the sacrifice.

Cadmus' men grabbed their pitchers and headed up to the spring. The water there flowed out of a narrow crevice of rock, close packed with dense vegetation. As the men knelt down to fill their pitchers, a piercing shriek echoed around the rocks, and a great serpent slithered out from the foliage. Its scaly head rose up until it peered down upon the men. A golden crest gleamed on its head, while a three-forked tongue flickered between its sharp fangs. It spewed out its venomous breath in a choking cloud, then lashed out at the men as they gasped for air. Some men it snatched up in its deadly jaws, others it crushed to death in its coils. A few men managed to draw their swords and fight back, but their bronze blades bounced harmlessly off the dragon's scales. In a matter of moments, the brave men who had followed Cadmus across hundreds of miles had all been killed.

Meanwhile, Cadmus had finished his preparations for the sacrifice, and begun to worry that his friends had not returned. As the sun started down in the sky, Cadmus picked up his spear and his iron sword and started after them. When Cadmus reached the spring, he stared in horror at the carnage before him. His faithful companions lay in slaughtered heaps, their bodies torn and crushed. And there, in the midst of it all, the great dragon lay coiled, licking at the bloody wounds of the fallen.

Filled with rage, Cadmus cried out, "My loyal friends. I shall either avenge your deaths or become your companion!" Then, tearing a great rock from the ground, Cadmus flung it at the dragon. The rock shattered against the scaly hide. Once again, the dragon reared up, gave its shrieking cry, and lunged. Cadmus dodged aside, then drove his spear between the dragon's scales until the spear tip burst out of the serpent's back. The creature thrashed from side to side, ripping the spear from Cadmus' hands and shattering the handle, but the spearhead remained fixed in its spine. Then Cadmus drew his iron sword. He stabbed repeatedly at the creature's head, driving it back, until, with a mighty lunge, Cadmus drove the sword through the creature's throat and pinned it to a tree behind. For a moment the great serpent writhed in place, before it died upon the tree.

As the life faded from the dragon's eyes, the goddess Athena appeared beside Cadmus. She commanded the hero to cut out the dragon's teeth, give half of them to her, and then plant the rest in the ground like seeds. Cadmus did as he was instructed, then watched in amazement as armed men grew out of the ground where he had planted the teeth. Cadmus reached for his sword, but one of the newly born men told him to keep back and take no part in their affairs. So Cadmus just watched as these earth-born men attacked and killed one another, until only five remained. Then Athena appeared again and ordered the men to stop fighting and join with Cadmus. With these new companions, Cadmus went back to where the heifer had sat down. He made his sacrifice and founded a city with the help of his five companions. He named the city Thebes, and it would become one of the richest cities in the world.

ⱷ•ⱷ•ⱷ•ⱷ•ⱷ•ⱷ

Cadmus and the Dragon by Francesco Zuccarelli. (Rafael Valls Gallery / The Bridgeman Art Library)

The story of Cadmus, his battle with the dragon, and the founding of the city of Thebes can be found scattered throughout the works of the Ancient Greek and Roman writers including Apollonius, Apollodorus, and even Homer. Probably the most complete and coherent version of the story is presented in Ovid's *Metamorphoses*, from which the above version is mostly drawn.

In many versions of the story, the dragon killed by Cadmus was sacred to Ares, the god of war, and Cadmus is forced to serve the god for several years by way of restitution, before being allowed to return to Thebes and marry

JASON AND THE ARGONAUTS

Probably the most famous dragon in Ancient Greek myth and legend is the giant serpent that guards the Golden Fleece in the story of Jason and the Argonauts. In some versions of the tale, Jason does slay the dragon, but in most, the dragon is put to sleep, either by the witch Medea or by Orpheus the musician. To make matters slightly more confusing, the dragon teeth sown into the ground by Jason do not come from the guardian of the Golden Fleece, but instead are the other half of the teeth from the dragon slain by Cadmus which were taken by Athena.

This is not to say that Jason and the Argonauts are not dragonslayers. According to a Slovenian legend, Jason and the Argonauts battled with a dragon near a swampy river, on their journey back with the Golden Fleece. After slaying the dragon, Jason founded the city of Ljubljana, the modern capital of Slovenia. His feat is commemorated by a quartet of dragon statues that guard the corners of 'Dragon Bridge' in the center of Ljubljana.

The exact origin of this legend is unclear, but it almost certainly owes more to medieval city-founding legends than it does to the tales of Ancient Greece.

Apparently, in some versions of the story, Jason is not so successful when facing the dragon. In this ancient artwork, the goddess Athena commands the dragon to regurgitate the unfortunate Argonaut.

the goddess Harmonia. In this case, the story becomes a rare example of a tale in which the dragonslayer is actually punished for his victory. Also, some versions have Cadmus transformed into a dragon as punishment, while others say that the transformation occurred much later in his life, when he taunts the gods because of his ill luck. In either case, the story is one of the few that has a dragonslayer himself becoming a dragon.

Thankfully, the story of Cadmus generally ends happily, with Zeus taking Cadmus and his wife, Harmonia, away to the Elysian Fields.

These days, Cadmus is more often mentioned for his other mythical endeavor, the introduction of the Phoenician alphabet to Greece as told by Herodotus in his *Histories*. Cadmus the dragonslayer is mostly forgotten; his legend overshadowed by those of the later Greek heroes, most notably by the greatest Greek hero of them all, the dragonslayer Hercules.

Hercules and Ladon, the Hundred-headed Dragon

Statue of Hercules and Ladon outside of Waldstein Palace in Prague.

For eight long years, Greece's greatest hero, Hercules, had labored as a servant for King Eurystheus, a punishment for the murder of his own sons in a fit of madness. Early in his servitude, Eurystheus had ordered Hercules to kill the Lernaean Hydra, a terrible dragon-like creature with nine heads, eight mortal ones, and one immortal, all of which breathed a poisonous breath. Riding the chariot of his comrade Iolaus to the creature's lair, Hercules forced it to emerge by hurling flaming brands into its cave. He then charged the monster and battered off several of the hydra's heads with his mighty club, but for every head he severed, two more quickly grew in its place. So in the midst of the fight, he commanded Iolaus to take up a burning brand and sear the stumps of the heads as he battered them off. This kept them from regrowing. Eventually, only the immortal head remained. Hercules tore off this last head with his bare hands, buried it in the ground, and placed a great boulder on top of it. He then ripped open the hydra's body and soaked his arrows in its deadly, venomous blood.

Many years had passed since that fight, and many deeds had been accomplished. In that time Hercules had killed the Erymanthian Boar, captured a golden-horned stag, defeated the triple-bodied Geryon, and taken the belt of Hippolyta, queen of the Amazons. He even wrestled with Cerberus, the three-headed dog that guarded Hades, and defeated the creature despite the sting of its dragon-like tail. Recently, he had joined with the Argonauts on their quest to recover the Golden Fleece, before they had abandoned him on the journey.

Now, one last task remained to him, one last labor to secure his freedom. King Eurystheus had commanded him to fetch the golden apples of the Hesperides, which were guarded by Ladon, a dragon with one hundred heads. And so Hercules set out alone, so that no one could accuse him of having received help in this, his final task. He took with him only his great club, his bow and the deadly arrows soaked in hydra blood. He dressed in the skin of the Nemean Lion, which he had slain. By ship, he crossed the Mediterranean to Libya and then traveled on foot through the Atlas Mountains. Without food or water, he journeyed under the sun's cruel heat, until he stood on a peak above the Garden of the Hesperides.

With a grim face, cracked with thirst, Hercules strung his bow and marched down into the garden. From his quiver, he drew a long arrow, its head stained with the poison of the hydra, and set it in his bow. In the garden ahead, he spied his enemy coiled around the tree of golden apples, its long serpentine body ending in a waving mass of long-necked dragonheads. Each head called with a different voice, producing a painful cacophony, a swirling storm of language. By willpower, Hercules blocked out the sound. He raised his bow to his eye, drew back the bowstring to his ear and loosed. The arrow streaked out and exploded through the writhing mass of heads, severing two, and causing the dragon to rear back in pain. Again and again, Hercules nocked his arrows, drew back the bowstring, and let fly. His shafts buried deep in the dragon's body. It crawled forward, but under the barrage of arrows, each soaked in deadly poison, it wavered then fell. It crashed down amongst the trees of the garden, and its heads fell silent.

Hercules neither smiled nor frowned at the destruction he had brought to the garden. Without a word, he walked past the dying dragon and found the golden apples he'd come to fetch. He would return them to King Eurystheus, and then he would once again be free to chart his own destiny.

ↄ·ↄ·ↄ·ↄ·ↄ·ↄ

It is impossible to write a history of dragonslayers without covering Hercules, and yet he is one of the most confusing and controversial heroes to claim the title. For most heroes, their fight with a dragon is their defining moment, the deed that grants them legendary status. But Hercules is a hero without equal, a demi-god who accomplished so many feats and who slew so many monsters that no one story, no one deed, defines him. Thus, many of his triumphs are only recorded briefly and details are lacking.

Many would probably state that his slaying of the Lernaean Hydra earns him the title of dragonslayer. Certainly the beast had many dragon-like qualities: a mass of snake-like heads, poison breath and it lived near water. However, others have argued that a hydra is a distinct type of creature, similar, but separate to dragons. The fact that it is called the *Lernaean* Hydra, lends evidence to the argument.

Hercules Killing the Dragon of the Garden of the Hesperides by Juan Bautista Martinz de Mazo. (Master Pics / Alamy)

Even if the hydra is discounted from the argument, Hercules also slew Ladon, who is more obviously a dragon. Or did he? Probably the most famous "biography" of Hercules, the one contained in Apollodorus' *Library*, states that Hercules never even saw the dragon, but convinced the Titan Atlas to fetch the apples for him. The only other complete life of Hercules that has been handed down from the Ancient world, that found in Diodorus Siculus' *Library of History*, states absolutely that Hercules did kill the guardian of the golden apples, but adds that the "dragon" might have been a shepherd named "Dracon," which is rather less than heroic.

Still, there are other writings that argue more in his favor. The first century Roman writer, Gaius Julius Hyginus, states unequivocally in his *Fabulae* that Hercules killed the huge dragon Ladon. Interestingly, the best evidence, and the most complete account of the encounter between Hercules and Ladon, is found in Apollonius of Rhodes' *Argonautica*. In this book, Jason and the Argonauts come across the still-twitching body of Ladon, the day after the dragon was killed by their former shipmate, Hercules.

So, while many of the myths and legends surrounding Hercules are confusing or contradictory, there is probably more evidence to support his claim to the title of dragonslayer than there is for many other heroes, and to leave him out of such a discussion would leave a gaping hole in the record.

As a final piece of evidence, let us look at one more story that is relatively consistent amongst the chroniclers. When Hercules was eight months old, a pair of large serpents crawled into his bed, intent on murder. Instead of showing fear, the babe leapt up, grabbed a serpent in either hand and strangled them both. Surely there is no greater foreshadowing for the life of a dragonslayer...

MARCUS ATILIUS REGULUS

In the first half of the third century BCE, Marcus Atilius Regulus led a Roman expedition against Carthage. In a story told by the Roman historians Livy and Cassius Dio (as related by John of Damascus), as the Roman Army was fighting against the Carthaginians, a great dragon attacked them from the River Bagradas. The dragon caused havoc, tearing soldiers apart with its mouth and crushing others with its tail. When the Romans realized that their javelins couldn't penetrate the dragon's hide, they brought up catapults and battered the dragon to death with a barrage of heavy stones.

Marcus Atilius Regulus ordered his soldiers to skin the dragon and sent its hide back to Rome as proof of their victory. The skin was 120 feet long.

Daniel of the Lion's Den

By the time Cyrus the Great became king in Babylon, Daniel was nearly one hundred years old. His body had bent with age and his eyes were failing him, but his mind was as sharp as ever. The people still held him in great respect for his wisdom, and often repeated the story of his long survival in the lion's den. The new king, however, paid him little attention.

That is until, one day, the king was walking outside the temple of Bel, a god worshipped by many in Babylon. He saw Daniel standing outside the temple, and asked him why he did not go in. Daniel responded, "Because I do not revere idols made with human hands."

The king furrowed his brow and said, "You do not think Bel is a living god? Have you seen how much food he eats and how much wine he drinks every night?"

Daniel laughed. "Do not be deceived, my king. It is only bronze on the outside and clay on the inside. It has never eaten a morsel or drunk a drop."

At this response Cyrus grew angry. "Then say who deceives me, and I will have them killed, but if you cannot, then I shall have you killed instead."

"Let it be as you say," agreed Daniel, and together they entered the temple. The great idol of Bel sat in the midst of the temple, cold and lifeless, while a great feast was spread out in offering before him.

"See this food?" said the king. "See this wine? If it is not Bel who eats it, then who can it be?"

"Send away the priests," said Daniel softly. Once the priests had left, Daniel had a servant fetch a bowl of ashes, and the two of them spread the ashes around the floor. Then, with the king, they locked the temple doors.

In the morning, King Cyrus and Daniel met at the doors to the temple. The king showed Daniel that they were still locked shut and no one could have got inside. Daniel just nodded as the doors were unlocked and thrown open.

The food had been eaten. The wine had been drunk. Only bones and scraps remained of the great feast that had been set before Bel.

"See," cried Cyrus, "Bel has feasted!"

"Look at the floor, my good king," said Daniel.

The king gazed at the floor and saw dozens of footprints in the ashes. He followed the tracks backwards and discovered a secret door, concealed within the altar.

"Every night," Daniel explained, "the priests come through this door and consume the food that has been left for Bel." The king, angered at this deception, immediately ordered the priests rounded up and executed.

Afterwards, the king summoned Daniel. "You are wise, Daniel, as the people say. Bel was a false idol indeed. But what of the dragon that so many of the people of Babylon worship? Surely it is a worthy god? I have seen it eat and drink with my own eyes."

"Indeed it is a mighty beast," admitted Daniel, "but it is no immortal god. Give me permission, and I will slay this creature without sword or club."

At this the king laughed. "You have my permission."

Then Daniel went off and gathered together pitch, fat, and hair, all of which he baked together and made into cakes. These he took with him, when

Another depiction of Daniel killing the Babylonian dragon. (Mary Evans Picture Library / Alamy)

he met the king in front of the temple that the Babylonians had built for their dragon god. King Cyrus and Daniel entered together, and saw the fearsome beast chained within. It saw them too, roaring and snapping at the two men as they drew closer.

"Without sword or club," reminded the king.

Daniel smiled and pulled out his cakes. These he tossed up and watched as the dragon greedily snatched them from the air. For a second, nothing happened. Then the dragon's stomach began to swell as the fire in its belly got hold of the cakes. The king and Daniel backed away as the dragon screamed its agony, until its stomach burst in a bright shower of flames and flesh. Then the dragon crashed to the ground, dead.

"Surely this creature was no god, nor was Bel," said the king. "Your eyes may be old, friend Daniel, but they see more than mine. I will keep you beside me always and listen to your counsel."

ᥫ᭡·ᥫ᭡·ᥫ᭡·ᥫ᭡·ᥫ᭡·ᥫ᭡

Cú Chulainn

The son of the Celtic god Lugh and a mortal mother, Cú Chulainn remains the greatest of all Irish mythical heroes. Although the story of his life is scattered through Irish, Scottish and Manx folklore, his list of deeds and battles rivals even the great Hercules. Cú Chulainn was a warrior of the highest order, who wielded the magical spear *Gáe Bulg*, and often flew into an unstoppable berserker rage in battle.

In one ancient tale called *Fled Bricrenn* (Bricriu's Feast), part of the group of stories known as the Ulster Cycle, Cú Chulainn is drawn into a competition to see who should receive the 'Champions Portion' of the feast. During the test to determine the champion, a gigantic serpent attacks Cú Chulainn. Undaunted, Cú Chulainn leaps upon the beast and rips its heart out with his bare hands. So great were the deeds of this hero, that the mere slaying of a dragon while unarmed is only mentioned briefly.

Cú Chulainn does have one other dubious, if highly relevant distinction. He is perhaps the only dragonslayer to have killed another dragonslayer. During his greatest adventure, the *Táin Bó Cúailnge* (The Cattle Raid of Cooley), Cú Chulainn single-handedly defies an army by continuously challenging its champions to one-on-one combat at the ford of a river. Amongst the numerous warriors and heroes that he kills is a young demi-god named Fráech.

The son of the Celtic goddess Bébinn and a mortal man, Fráech battled a giant serpent while trying to win the hand of the beautiful Findabair. Although he slew the dragon, he was so badly wounded in the fight that it took a hundred and fifty maidens of the Sidhe to heal him. Fráech eventually married Findabair and lived many happy years before meeting Cú Chulainn in the river ford.

The story of Bel and the dragon is found in book 14 of *Daniel* in both Catholic and Orthodox bibles. It is not, however, found in the Hebrew *Torah*, nor in most Protestant bibles. The story comes from a group of ancient writings that are collectively known as either the *Apocrypha* (to Anglicans) or the *Deuterocanonical* books (to Catholics). Because these books are part of the *Old Testament*, but do not appear in the *Torah*, they have been the source of great debate among Christians since the very earliest days of the Bible's existence.

Regardless of its theological importance, the story is also interesting for historical and literary reasons. Historically, it argues that Daniel was still alive in 559 BCE, when Cyrus became king of the Persians. Unlike many of his contemporaries, Cyrus the Great, as he became known, proved to be a liberal and tolerant ruler, especially when it came to religion. His thirty-year rule saw the founding of the Achaemenid Empire, which would famously go to war with Greece a hundred years or so later. In the world of literature, the story of Bel is often cited as the first "locked room" mystery, a theme that is now ubiquitous in mystery writing.

Although Daniel's encounter with the dragon is recounted in just six lines in the Bible, it is a story that has had a far-reaching effect in the history of the dragonslayer legend. The idea of killing a dragon by feeding it something deadly and explosive reoccurs numerous times in myth and legend. Most famously it is employed by Skuba, the Polish boy who kills the Wawel Dragon in Krakow and by the young Scottish cinder boy, Assipattle, who uses the strategy to kill the Mester Stoor Worm.

NORSE DRAGONSLAYERS

Although the word "dragon" derives from the Ancient Greek, the modern European conception of the nature of a dragon owes more to the shared heroic mythology of the Ancient Norse, Germans and Anglo-Saxons. In these legends, set in the tumultuous period known as the Dark Ages, dragons, or wyrms as they are usually called, are still most often depicted as giant serpents. However, in the two most important tales, those of Sigurd and Beowulf, the dragons take on much more recognizable forms. Sigurd battles a dragon that drags its ponderous bulk around on four legs, while Beowulf's foe can fly and breathe fire. Merged into one, these two wyrms combine to create the definitive winged, four-legged, fire-breathing beast that most modern readers would recognize as the form of a dragon.

Also from the Norse legends comes the idea of dragons as guardians of treasure hoards. In a couple of tales, the treasure is a princess, but in most it is a pile of gold, jewels, and weaponry. Dragons had become the living embodiments of greed and miserliness. While in today's society these sins are viewed as just two of many, to the ancient Norse they were the greatest of all failings. Norse society was based around the warband and functioned only through a warlord generously sharing his treasure with his followers. A man who hoarded his wealth threatened to undermine the structure and power of his clan. Thus dragons were more than just dangerous beasts; they were forces of chaos and destruction, who threatened to bring all society to ruin.

Only the greatest heroes could stand before a dragon. Presented here are the stories of the two most famous Norse heroes, Sigurd the Völsung and Beowulf.

Sigurd the Völsung

Sigurd was born into a blood feud; for while he was still in the womb, King Lyngvi and his brothers fought against Sigurd's father, Sigmund. During the battle, the god Odin shattered Sigmund's blade and killed him. Sigurd's mother, Hjördis, recovered the broken blade and fled to the court of King Hjalprek in Denmark. In this safe haven, she gave birth to Sigurd, the last of the great family of Völsungs.

Siegfried (or Sigurd) slaying Fáfnir. The depiction of Siegfried dressed in skins owes more to the later idea of the "noble barbarian" than to the original stories.

(Opposite) Sigurd slaying Fáfnir. While most modern depictions of Sigurd/Sigfried show the hero wearing primitive skins, this artwork presents him in the dress and armor appropriate to a Germanic warrior of the sixth century.

As a young man, Sigurd excelled in all Viking pursuits: sports, chess, the reading of runes, and, of course, feats of arms. In order to further Sigurd's education, the king assigned a blacksmith named Reginn to serve as his tutor and foster-father. While Reginn taught the young Sigurd many lessons, the smith held a dark family secret that drove him toward wickedness.

One day, when Sigurd was just coming into the strength of manhood, Reginn taunted him about his lack of wealth. Sigurd's father, Sigmund, had possessed riches fit for a king, but all he had left for his son was a broken sword. Then Reginn said he knew a place where Sigurd could acquire a vast treasure, wealth that would earn him the respect of everyone. When Sigurd asked him how he knew of such a treasure, Reginn told him the story of his family, and the birth of the dragon, Fáfnir.

Reginn was the youngest of three sons. His oldest brother, Fáfnir, was a rough and greedy man, while his second brother, Ötr, was a gentle soul. Ötr had the ability to transform himself into an otter, and spent his days fishing in the local river. Once, while fishing, the gods Odin, Hœnir, and Loki walked by the river. They saw Ötr fishing in his otter form, and Loki killed him with a rock. The gods then skinned the otter and continued on their way. When they came to the house of Reginn's father, the gods discovered their mistake. Reginn's father demanded that the gods pay a blood-price, enough treasure to completely cover the poor otter's skin and stuff its body. So Odin sent Loki to get the treasure. Loki, the trickster god, took the treasure from a dwarf named Andvari, but not before the dwarf placed a curse over all of the gold, and, in particular, on a golden ring. The mischievous Loki brought the treasure back to Odin, but told no one about the curse. Odin covered the otter's skin with the gold, but missed a single whisker. When the whisker was pointed out, Odin covered it with the cursed golden ring. Then the gods went on their way.

Thus, in a single night, Reginn's family became one of the richest in the land, but the curse of the gold struck quickly. Fáfnir, ever greedy, murdered his father and fled with the treasure. He built himself a great lair, sunk into the earth and protected with an iron door. In this dungeon, he would sleep on top of his pile of gold. Slowly, through the evil in his own heart and the obsession with the power to protect his hoard, Fáfnir transformed into a monstrous wyrm, a creature of greed and venomous poison.

When Reginn told this tale to Sigurd, the young Völsung declared that he would kill the dragon, but first he must have a proper sword. Reginn made him a sword, but when Sigurd struck it against the anvil, it shattered. Reginn made him a second sword, but this too shattered on the anvil. After this had

In order to win the hand of the beautiful Brynhildr, potential suitors were required to ride through a ring of fire. Although Sigurd accomplished the feat in the guise of his brother-in-law, Gunnar, he is clearly identified in this image by his dragon helm.

happened several times, Sigurd went to his mother and asked for the pieces of his father's sword, which she gladly gave to him. He took the pieces to Reginn, who re-forged them into a new sword. Fire danced from the blade as Sigurd swung this new sword for the first time. Then he tested it against the anvil and split the solid block of metal in half. Sigurd named the sword Gram.

Sigurd declared that with this sword, he could kill the mighty wyrm, but, first, he had his own debt to settle. With the aid of King Hjalprek, Sigurd assembled an army of warriors. Then he sailed across the sea to attack his father's killers. In a series of bloody battles, Sigurd struck down all of his foes and won great renown. He returned to Denmark a true Viking warrior.

Soon after Sigurd returned, Reginn found him and reminded him of his promise to kill Fáfnir. The next day, the two men rode out together in search of the wyrm. For several days, Reginn led them through empty lands, and then up into the lonely heath. There they spied a track of dead plants and worn earth that led down to a stagnant pool of water. Seeing the size of the path, and the breadth of the destruction around it, Sigurd wondered at the size of the beast, but Reginn told him not to fear. He suggested that Sigurd dig a pit in the ground, where he could hide until the dragon passed over. Then he could attack the monster from beneath.

Having proposed the plan, Reginn rode off to hide, while Sigurd dug the ditch. As Sigurd was digging, Odin came walking down the road in the disguise of an old man with a long beard. Seeing Sigurd's plan, he suggested the young warrior dig a series of ditches, so that the wyrm's blood could flow freely and not drown Sigurd in his ditch. Sigurd saw wisdom in this and did as was suggested, but when he went to thank the old man, Odin had vanished.

Eventually, Sigurd finished his digging and crouched down in his ditch. For a while he waited on the empty heath, with just the rustle of the wind in the scrub to keep him company. Then he heard a distant pounding and felt a tremor in the earth. Steadily the noise grew, as did the shaking of the ground. Fáfnir approached; crawling low on four heavy legs, the mighty wyrm spewed a cloud of poison before him, withering the plants down to their roots. As the great creature's bulk passed over the ditch, Sigurd drove Gram up under his left shoulder, stabbing the blade up to its hilt in the wyrm's flesh. Blood poured down on Sigurd, soaking his clothes, but enough ran off into the other ditches to keep him from drowning in the vile fluid.

Fáfnir thrashed his long neck and tail, gouging the earth and tearing up plants, roaring out the pain of his mortal wound. When he finally saw Sigurd crawl out from his ditch, the wyrm had no strength left to fight and could feel his life slipping away. With his last breaths, the dragon advised Sigurd to ride away from this place, to leave the treasure untouched. If Sigurd took the treasure, Fáfnir promised a great doom would find him. With that, the mighty wyrm died.

Sigurd pulled Gram out of the dragon's body and wiped the bloody blade on the grass. As he finished, Reginn rode up and looked upon the dead monster with greedy eyes. He asked of Sigurd, since it was he that had forged the blade that killed the mighty wyrm, if he could have the honor of eating its heart. Sigurd agreed and even offered to cook it for him.

As Sigurd roasted the dragon's heart over an open flame, he touched it with a finger to see if it was cooked. Then he stuck the finger in his mouth and tasted the dragon's blood. Suddenly, he could understand the speech of the birds, and he heard four of them talking nearby. They said that Reginn planned to eat the heart to gain wisdom and the power of prophecy, and then would murder Sigurd to get the treasure. Better, said the birds, that Sigurd should eat the heart himself and kill his treacherous companion. Sigurd looked over at Reginn and saw the truth in his eyes. So Sigurd drew Gram and struck off Reginn's head. Then he ate the heart himself. Leaving behind the bodies of Reginn and Fáfnir, Sigurd rode on to the dragon's den and found all of his gold and treasure. Unconcerned by the threats of the curse, he loaded everything onto his horse and rode home.

The story of Sigurd and his victory over Fáfnir spread far and wide, but already his doom closed around the young warrior. Soon he met and fell in love with a warrior woman named Brynhildr, and the two pledged themselves to one another. But Sigurd was soon called away, and in his travels he came to the court of Gjúki, who had a wife, three sons, and a daughter. Gjúki's wife, Grimhild, determined that Sigurd should marry her daughter, Gudrun, so she made a potion of forgetfulness, which she gave to Sigurd. The young warrior immediately forgot about Brynhildr, and agreed to marry Gudrun.

Still the curse of the treasure haunted Sigurd for, some time later, his new brother-in-law, Gunnar, asked Sigurd's help in winning Brynhildr for his bride. Without recognizing his former love, Sigurd disguised himself as Gunnar, and tricked Brynhildr into marrying him. Eventually, Brynhildr discovered the truth of both the disguise and of the potion, and plotted her revenge. She told Gunnar that Sigurd slept with her while disguised as him. Gunnar, incensed, enchanted his younger brother, causing him to go berserk and murder Sigurd in his sleep. Byrnhildr also murdered the three-year-old son of Sigurd and Gudrun.

Destroyed by her despair, Brynhildr built a funeral pyre for Sigurd and his son, then threw herself into the flames.

ෆ•ෆ•ෆ•ෆ•ෆ•ෆ

Another depiction of the barbarian Siegfried slaying Fáfnir. (Photo 12 / Alamy)

The story of Sigurd the dragonslayer forms a major part of *The Saga of the Völsungs*, a short work written by an unknown Icelandic author sometime between 1200 and 1270 CE. Although the saga is based on an earlier poetic tradition, only some of these poems have survived to the present.

The saga describes the mythical founding of the family of Völsungs, and then follows the family through its generations of heroes, ending with Sigurd, the last and greatest of the Völsungs. Because many of the characters in the saga can be connected to historical figures from the fifth and sixth centuries, figures such as Attila the Hun, scholars have spent many years looking for the historical Sigurd. Perhaps the most likely candidate for a real Sigurd is the Frankish King Sigibert, who lived between 535 and 575 CE and ruled a large area of what is now northern France and Belgium. Sigibert married a Visigothic princess named Brunhilda, before being murdered by assassins hired by his brother's wife. While the circumstantial evidence of the similar names and the similar end is compelling, it is far from convincing proof.

Another intriguing piece of the Sigurd puzzle is found in *Beowulf*, the other great Norse dragonslaying story. Early on, this poem mentions Sigemund the Wælsing, who killed a dragon, guardian of the treasure hoard. Sigemund the Wælsing is the Anglo-Saxon version of Sigmund Völsung, the father of Sigurd. While acknowledging the possibility that Sigmund and Sigurd were both dragonslayers, it seems more likely that at some point this deed of Sigmund was somehow transferred to his son Sigurd, as *Beowulf* was written first.

Whatever the truth behind the Sigurd legend, its longevity and influence is beyond question. Over the centuries, the original Icelandic manuscript was copied over and over, and numerous handwritten examples still survive today. While the story would prove hugely influential in Germany during the Middle Ages (see sidebar on Siegfried), it wasn't until the nineteenth century that the story began to enter into the consciousness of the English-speaking world. In the 1870s, one of the earliest fantasy writers, William Morris, rewrote the story in a 10,000-line epic poem called *The Story of Sigurd the Volsung and the Fall of the Niblungs*. Although the poem received a good critical reception, its length and the difficulty of its language kept it from widespread popularity.

Undoubtedly, the greatest effect of the Sigurd legend on the modern English reader comes through its influence on J.R.R. Tolkien, the most important writer of modern dragonslaying stories. The legend of Sigurd serves as a direct influence for his story of the dragonslayer, Túrin Tarmbar, in *The Children of Húrin*, but also provides important elements in his more famous works, *The Hobbit* and *The Lord of the Rings*. *The Hobbit* features a dragonslayer, Bard the Bowman, who understands the language of birds and who kills a dragon that sleeps atop a pile of Dwarven treasure. While *The Lord of the Rings* doesn't contain a dragon, it does have a broken magical sword that is remade and, of course, a cursed magical ring.

SIEGFRIED

Germany's greatest legendary hero, the dragonslayer Siegfried, is the star of a medieval heroic epic, a series of famous operas and a controversial pair of silent films. Although the story of Siegfried grows out of the same legendary tradition that spawned Sigurd, it has, in the ensuing centuries, taken on a life of its own.

The story of the Siegfried legend begins in the early thirteenth century, when an unknown German poet wrote a manuscript now known as *Das Nibelungenlied* (*The Lay of the Nibelungs*). A heroic epic set in a semi-mythical Dark Ages Europe, *Das Nibelungenlied* tells the story of the young warrior Siegfried (sometimes translated as Sifrit), his courtship and marriage to the beautiful princess Kriemhild, and his downfall due to the machinations of the warrior-woman Brünhild. It then relates the bloody revenge extracted by Kriemhild for her murdered husband. Although Siegfried's battle with the dragon is not shown in the story, it does form a vital part of the plot. In this tale, Siegfried killed the dragon while still young and then bathed in his blood to make himself invulnerable to all weapons. However, while bathing, a single leaf stuck to his back and left one spot vulnerable. It is the revelation of this weakness that allows Siegfried's murderer to succeed.

Das Nibelungenlied proved a popular story in the early centuries of the German Middle Ages and today forty or so manuscripts or fragments survive. The story's popularity seems to have waned with the passing centuries, and appears to have all but disappeared from the German consciousness by the sixteenth century. Although both the manuscripts and the story itself would be 'rediscovered' in the eighteenth century, it wasn't until it came into the hands of the famous composer Richard Wagner that Siegfried would once again achieve legendary status.

Over the space of twenty-six years, Wagner used *Das Nibelungenlied* (and much of the Sigurd legend) to construct a cycle of four operas collectively known as *Der Ring des Nibelungen*. This fifteen-hour operatic masterpiece charts the history of a cursed ring, which eventually ends up in the hands of Siegfried, leading to his betrayal and murder and eventually the destruction of the entire world. The full cycle was first performed in 1876, at an opera house in Bayreuth built specifically for the occasion and designed by Wagner himself.

The success of the Opera caused a resurgence of interest in the story of Siegfried, and slowly the legend became linked with German nationalism (even though the Siegfried in *Das Nibelungenlied* is actually Dutch). In 1923 the Austrian director Fritz Lang brought the legend to the silver screen with a two-part adaptation *Die Nibelungen: Siegfried* and *Die Nibelungen: Kriemhilds Rache* (*Kriemhild's Revenge*). Considered a classic of the era, the movie featured a twenty-metre long dragon model controlled by operators inside and beneath it.

In the lead-up to World War II, the Nazi Party used both the opera and the movie as propaganda tools, and there was even a movement by some to replace Christianity with a new religion based around the idea of Siegfried as a sun god. Some of this taint has remained attached to the legend of Siegfried in the twenty-first century, but, among many, he has rightfully reclaimed his place both as a legendary hero and one of the best-known dragonslayers.

A still of Siegfried fighting Fafnir from the 1923 silent movie. (Photo 12 / Alamy)

Beowulf

For nearly fifty years, Beowulf had ruled as king of the Geats. To the Swedes and Danes, he was a living legend, for in his youth he had sailed with a band of companions to Heorot, the hall of King Hrothgar. There he battled a ferocious ogre called Grendel, who would break into the hall at night and snatch men to eat. Within the walls of Heorot, the man and ogre wrestled, as swords could not harm the beast, until Beowulf grabbed the monster's arm and tore it from his shoulder. The wounded beast ran off into the night, gushing blood from the ragged stump of its shoulder.

The severed arm had been nailed to the wall as a symbol of victory, and the next day all of the people of Heorot rejoiced and feasted. King Hrothgar gave out treasure aplenty, most generously to Beowulf himself, but the danger had not ended. That night, as Beowulf slept away from his companions, another monster slipped into the hall: Grendel's mother, come to avenge her son.

Beowulf takes cover behind his iron shield. (Ivy Close Images / Alamy)

That vile ogress snatched up a man while he was sleeping and murdered him without a thought. When the alarm was raised, she fled away into the night, taking the body with her.

In the morning, Beowulf organized his men and set off after the creature. They journeyed through the empty moors until they came to a dreary wood, surrounding a blood-red lake. There they found the severed head of their missing companion lying on the shore. All around the dark sinkhole, serpents and small sea-dragons slithered and swam. They dove into the lake as the warriors approached, but Beowulf snatched up his bow and sent a barbed arrow streaking out. It pierced one of the loathsome serpents in the vitals. The monster tumbled into the water, where Beowulf's men finished it off with boar-spears. They dragged its carcass up onto the shore and gazed in morbid disgust at the dragonish creature.

Then Beowulf donned his armor and drew his sword. With final words of parting, he approached the bloody caldron of the lake and dove in. He intended to let the weight of his armor carry him down to the monster's lair on the bottom, but Grendel's mother was alerted by the sounds of fighting. She grabbed Beowulf, pinning his arms by his sides, and dragging him toward her lair. All around him, the vicious dragon-things bit and gouged at his armor, while the ogress pulled him along. In a moment, they had emerged into a dank underground cave, the lair of the beast. Beowulf struggled to his feet and struck out with his sword. The blade rebounded without a scratch against the head of the monstrous killer. The sword clattered aside, and so Beowulf tried to throttle the creature. The ogress threw him to the ground then dove on top of him with her dagger drawn. There his life would have ended if not for his armor, but his mail turned her blade aside.

Then Beowulf spied another sword, lying among the creature's hoard of stolen treasure. It was a sword of giants, double-edged and razor-sharp, forged in another age. Few men now could lift its weight, but Beowulf snatched it

Wiglaf brings the treasure from the dragon's cave. (Mary Evans Picture Library / Alamy)

up, and swung that mighty blade. It sheared through the neck of the ogress, severing her head in a spray of blood. The head rolled near the body of her son, who lay dead in a corner. Beowulf then cut off Grendel's head as well, to prove that the creature was dead. With the heads of the two monsters, and the hilt of the sword, whose blade had melted in their blood, Beowulf returned to his companions and, eventually, to the hall of Heorot.

But five decades or more had passed since all of that. Now the aged king, Beowulf, stood on a hilltop and watched as distant flames consumed both his own hall and the village of his people. For hours he had watched in helpless heartache as a fire-drake, a winged-wyrm, had rained fire and destruction down on his people. The world of the Geats was being reduced to cinder and ash.

His warriors had caught the man who had started it all: a foolish thief who had stolen a golden cup from the dragon's hoard, enraging the vengeful beast. The thief would now be their guide back to the dragon's lair, where Beowulf would face his last and greatest battle. He glanced at his companions, all young men and untested in battle; they would be of little help. Beowulf had his smiths bring him a giant shield of iron that could turn aside the dragon's breath. He strapped the heavy shield upon his time-wearied arm, and nodded for the thief to lead the way.

The thirteen men walked long through the night, the distant fires shining like small candles. In time, they approached the rocky hills. The thief pointed towards a dark archway, the mouth of the dragon's cave. A small stream of fire trickled out of its open maw, confirming that the master of the hoard was home.

Beowulf ordered his companions to stay where they were; he would face the dragon alone. Drawing a time-tested sword, and walking with his shield held before him, he followed the burning stream up to the mound. Near the entrance, he stood his ground, and let out a mighty battle-roar. The challenging cry echoed from the cliffs and around the stones before the cave mouth. Then a lance of fire jetted out of the cave, and Beowulf caught it on his shield. In a cloud of choking smoke, the dragon emerged, a sinewy, black-scaled monster, covered in the filth of years. It belched forth another blast of flame, which spilled around the iron shield, singeing Beowulf's helmet and armor.

Then the two combatants, man and monster, rushed together. In a fury of sword, fang and claw, they struck at one another, clashing against shield and scales, but neither could gain the upper hand. They drew apart, the dragon drooling fire, the old king panting in the smoke-thick air.

All around, Beowulf's men shrank back from this fight, and fled into the woods. All but one; a young warrior called Wiglaf felt a stirring in his heart. Drawing his own blade, he rushed into the fray. Though never before had he weathered the battle-storm, he bellowed his own war cry as he charged into battle.

Undaunted by the appearance of a second foe, the dragon spat forth its flaming breath. The flames consumed Wiglaf's shield, burning it from his arm. He cast the smouldering ruins aside and took shelter behind the great iron shield of Beowulf. Then those two bold warriors moved forward together, striking at the dragon with their gleaming swords. The dragon sprang forward again, its claws screeching against the iron shield. Beowulf batted aside those fearful claws and brought his blade around to slash against the dragon's head. But, in that moment, the venerable sword shattered against the dragon's rock-hard scales.

For a stunned moment, Beowulf gazed at the broken blade in sad amazement. That instant of inattention proved fatal, for the dragon coiled its long neck around the shield and clamped its jaws around Beowulf's throat. Its fangs pierced the flesh of his neck and lifted him off the ground.

As the dragon reared up with the aged king trapped in its jaws, it exposed its vulnerable underbelly. With a cry of hatred, Wiglaf lunged forward, driving his sword deep into the dragon's belly. At the same moment, Beowulf drew a dagger from his belt, and, still suspended in the dragon's mouth, he plunged the knife into the creature's eye. Twice mortally wounded, the dragon dropped Beowulf to the ground and tumbled backwards in agony. Its fiery breath sprayed in all directions, then went out. It collapsed in a loathsome heap, smoking from its own dying fire.

With the dragon dead, Beowulf struggled to his feet, but his neck was already swelling from the bite of those poisoned fangs. He staggered to a seat by the entrance of the cave, his body clenching in agony. He spoke to Wiglaf through bloodied teeth and asked him to bring the treasures of the dragon before him. Wiglaf went into the dragon's lair, and found more treasure than an army could carry. He selected some of the best golden cups and gleaming jewels. These he brought back out and placed before his dying lord.

Beowulf smiled and removed his helmet. He gave the royal boar helm to young Wiglaf, his last act as a gift-giver. He commanded that the treasure be buried with him, to remove it from the temptation of thieves. Then with a final breath, Beowulf's eyes clouded over, and he passed from the world, the last of the great Geatish kings.

ᏩᎭᎤᎭᏩᎭᎤᎭᏩᎭᎤᎭ

It is only by the thinnest of margins and the greatest of luck that the story of Beowulf has survived to the present. It exists in only a single manuscript, now housed in the British Library. This manuscript was written in Old English by a pair of monks, many years apart. One started and wrote up to line 1939, the other finishing, sometime around 1000 CE. It is thought that they were copying an earlier version, possibly as old as the eighth century. By the eighteenth century, the all-but forgotten manuscript was part of the collection of Sir Robert Cotton. In 1731, a fire broke out in the collection, destroying over two hundred manuscripts. The Beowulf manuscript escaped with only

OTHER NORSE DRAGONSLAYERS

Ragnar Lodbrok

Ragnar 'Hairy-Breeks' or 'Hairy Britches' was a famous Viking who terrorized Europe in the ninth century and briefly claimed the throne of both Sweden and Denmark. In one famous tale, repeated in numerous folkloric and pseudo-historical sources, Ragnar fell in love with a young princess who lived in a tower completely encircled by a giant, two-legged serpent with a poisonous bite known as a lindworm. In order to battle the dragon, Ragnar dressed in some form of novel armor. In some versions it is a tunic covered in tar and sand, in others he wears a shaggy dress, which he soaks in water and allows to freeze, forming thick, icy plates. Either way, the extra protection allowed Ragnar to get close enough to pierce the worm with his spear and then cut off its head.

In some versions of the story, the rescued princess is named Thora. In others she is Aslaug, the daughter of Sigurd Völsung and Brynhildr, making Sigurd and Ragnar a rare father/son-in-law dragonslaying pair. Ragnar met his end in Northumbria, where he was captured after a shipwreck and thrown into a pit of poisonous vipers, or stabbed by an assassin wanting to frame the king of Northumbria, depending on which story you read.

Frotho I

According to the Danish historian and mythologist, Saxo Grammaticus, Frotho ruled Denmark after the death of his father King Hadingus. Through near constant military campaigning, Frotho emptied his treasury until nothing remained to pay his men. One day, while out riding and contemplating this problem, he overheard a farmer singing a song about a dragon that guarded a vast hoard of treasure. After questioning the farmer further about the beast, Frotho sailed out to a remote island, searching for the monster. He brought with him a special shield covered in the hide of a bull.

When he reached the island, Frotho soon discovered the dragon's tracks and decided to wait in ambush. It wasn't long before the scaly beast came slithering by. Frotho threw spears at the dragon, but saw them bounce of its armored body. Then, as it reared up, he remembered the farmer's parting comment. He looked carefully at the creature's lower body and saw a single spot, uncovered by scales. Frotho charged forward and plunged his sword into this unarmored spot, mortally wounding the dragon. Later, Frotho recovered the dragon's treasure and sailed home, more than able to fund his horde with the hoard.

Fridleif

Saxo Grammaticus tells a similar story about another legendary king of Denmark named Fridleif (or King Fridlevus II). In this tale, the Viking's ship was driven onto a deserted island, where Fridleif had a dream in which an old man (probably Odin) told him to dig up a treasure and fight a dragon. When he awoke, he was attacked by the dragon as it came out of the ocean. It uprooted trees with its long tail, while Fridleif's spears bounced off its scales. Then Fridleif attacked the creature at the point where its body touched the ground, and plunged his sword deep into its groin, killing it. He then recovered the treasure from an underground chamber and sailed home.

Ragnar Lodbrok is thrown into the pit of adders in this drawing by Richard Henry Brock. (The Stapleton Collection / The Bridgeman Art Library)

minor damage. The work received its first translations into modern English during the nineteenth century, and has since been under nearly continuous study as the only complete surviving example of Anglo-Saxon epic poetry. The story itself is set sometime during the fifth and sixth centuries, and, although a few of the minor characters can be connected with historical personages, no precise date for the story can be determined.

Just as important as Beowulf's contribution to the understanding of Old English literature is its place as arguably the single most important narrative in the history of the dragonslayer. With its flying, fire-breathing, treasure-hoarding dragon, the poem contains the most complete vision of a modern, Western European dragon. This description became even more strongly established when J.R.R. Tolkien used it as the basis for the dragon Smaug in *The Hobbit*. Not only that, but the poem also contains one of the few descriptions of an actual battle between a man and a dragon. In most stories, the battle itself is glossed over in a couple of words, while Beowulf carries the fight on for many gripping lines.

Despite being so instrumental in our modern conception of dragons and dragonslayers, the story is also unique in that it is perhaps the only dragonslayer story that features two warriors combining to kill the beast, as Wiglaf deserves just as much credit for the ultimate victory as does Beowulf. Also, it is a rare story in that the dragonslayer himself is also mortally wounded during the fight, perhaps displaying Anglo-Saxon leanings towards fatalism.

In the present day, the legend of Beowulf is mostly widely recognized due to a pair of movies, neither of which follow the plot of the story particularly closely. The first is *The 13th Warrior*, released in 1999, and based on the book *The Eaters of the Dead* by Michael Crichton. In this movie, the tenth-century historical figure Ahmad ibn Fadlan joins a group of Vikings who sail to Denmark in order to fight an unknown evil. The movie tries to put a "realistic" take on the Beowulf story, making Grendel a member of the last surviving tribe of Neanderthals, his mother the tribe's shaman, and the dragon or "fire-wyrm" a long line of torches carried by the tribe as they go to battle. The film proved to be both a critical and box office failure, although it remains popular with fans of bloody, medieval action adventure movies.

In 2007, director Robert Zemeckis used motion-capture to create a computer-animated version of Beowulf. Despite the cutting-edge effects, the movie plays fast and loose with the original story, presenting Grendel as a misunderstood child, and his mother as an evil seductress who sleeps with Beowulf and, by him, gives birth to the dragon. The film received mixed reviews, but did well at the box office.

Today, the story of Beowulf is still best enjoyed in its original poetic form, and a number of translations are available. The best-received translation of the last twenty years is probably the 1999 version by the Irish Nobel Laureate, Seamus Heaney.

(Opposite) Wiglaf receives Beowulf's helmet in this drawing by Hans W. Schmidt. (INTERFOTO / Alamy)

(Overleaf) *Beowulf and the Fire Drake*. The *Beowulf* dragon is the first example in European mythology of a fire-breathing dragon. Previously, most dragons had poisonous breath. This might be an early indication of Christianity creeping into the tale, using fire to connect the dragon to Satan, or, just as likely, it highlights the danger of fire at a time when nearly everything was constructed of wood.

Holy Dragonslayers

The Lord God said to the serpent, "Because you have done this, cursed are you above all livestock and above all beasts of the field; on your belly you shall go, and dust you shall eat all the days of your life. I will put enmity between you and the woman, and between your offspring and her offspring; he shall bruise your head, and you shall bruise his heel." Genesis 3:14–15

St. John the Evangelist, author of the Book of Revelation. In one of the stories of John, he is forced to drink from a poison cup but survives thanks to his faith in God. The poison is represented in this painting by the small dragon sitting on the edge of the cup.

From the earliest days of Christianity, serpents, and by extension dragons, have been viewed as the great evil, and as living embodiments of sin. Indeed, it was Satan, the devil himself, in the guise of the serpent that tricked Adam and Eve into eating the forbidden fruit for which they were expelled from the Garden of Eden. This act prompted God to make the pronouncement above, forever placing man and serpents as enemies.

The association between the devil and dragons is made even clearer in the twelfth book of Revelation:

And a great sign appeared in heaven: a woman clothed with the sun, with the moon under her feet, and on her head a crown of twelve stars. She was pregnant and was crying out in birth pains and the agony of giving birth. And another sign appeared in heaven: behold, a great red dragon, with seven heads and ten horns, and on his heads seven diadems. His tail swept down a third of the stars of heaven and cast them to the earth. And the dragon stood before the woman who was about to give birth, so that when she bore her child he might devour it. She gave birth to a male child, one who is to rule all the nations with a rod of iron, but her child was caught up to God and to his throne, and the woman fled into the wilderness, where she has a place prepared by God, in which she is to be nourished for 1,260 days. Now war arose in heaven, Michael and his angels fighting against the dragon. And the dragon and his angels fought back, but he was defeated, and there was no longer any place for them in heaven. And the great dragon was thrown down, that ancient serpent, who is called the devil and Satan, the deceiver of the whole world— he was thrown down to the earth, and his angels were thrown down with him. Revelation 12: 1–9

In this passage, the Archangel, St. Michael, becomes the prototype for warrior saints and especially for dragonslayers such as St. George. In fact, St. Michael and St. George are often seen depicted together in manuscripts and on stained glass windows.

Although the connection between dragons, Satan, sin and evil dates back to the earliest days of Christianity (and possibly even earlier), and many of the dragonslaying saints come from these early days of the Church, most of their dragon stories appear to be later medieval inventions. It may be that it wasn't until the Middle Ages that the rise in literacy rates allowed many of these stories to be written down. More likely, however, is that the stories developed with the spread of Christianity across Europe. The dragon, representing all things non-Christian, is often used as a metaphor for paganism. As Christianity spread into new regions, its preachers, the saints, pushed out the pagan dragons, and later medieval writers used this metaphor to explain the transition. This idea is most often associated with St. Patrick driving all of the snakes out of Ireland, but can easily be applied to many saintly dragonslaying stories.

Stained glass depiction of St. Michael slaying the Dragon of the Apocalypse from St. Michael's Church in Brampton, Cumbria, England. (Peter J. Hatcher / Alamy)

Today, it is impossible to say exactly how many stories exist of saints who slew, or in some fashion defeated, a dragon. Many are local tales that only survive in obscure collections, while, in other cases, saints are identified as dragonslayers, but the actual story has been lost. Western Christianity probably recognizes about fifty different saints who battled dragons; other branches of the religion could easily contain just as many, if not more.

Collected here are three legends of holy dragonslayers: St. George, the holy warrior; St. Sylvester, pope of the early Church; and St. Carantoc, an early Celtic saint who lived in the days of King Arthur.

St. George and the Dragon

St. George was born in Cappadocia, in the year 270 CE. His father was a city governor, while his mother was the daughter of a count and a descendant of Joseph of Arimathea, the bearer of the Holy Grail. While still a young man, George joined the legions of the Emperor Diocletian as a cavalry officer and fought in many battles. He served alongside the future emperor Constantine in both the Egyptian campaign of 295 CE and the Persian War from 297–299. During those days, both the Army and the Roman Empire were accepting of Christianity so, despite his faith, George rose steadily through the ranks, becoming one of Constantine's most trusted advisors.

After the battle of Satala in 298 CE once again brought peace to the Empire, Constantine, now a Tribune, dispatched George as a courier to Libya. When George arrived, he heard stories about a fearsome dragon that plagued the kingdom, destroying crops and killing livestock with its pestilential breath. In order to appease the dragon, the Libyans had offered it two sheep a day. As the sheep began to run out, the people sent their children instead, drawing lots to decide which child would go to sate the dragon's hunger. The week before George's arrival, the king's only daughter had drawn the cursed lot. The king begged his people to spare the princess, but they threatened to burn down his palace if he would not give the girl up. He then asked if the people would grant him one more week with his daughter before she was sent to the dragon, and to this they agreed.

And so it was that when George rode by the city of Silene, he found the young princess, dressed in her royal finery, tied to a lonely stake near a lake. He immediately dismounted and cut the girl free of her bonds, but she refused to leave. She told George the story of the dragon and of her father and how, if she did not die, the people would burn down the palace. Struck by the young girl's courage, George vowed that he would defeat the dragon and save both her and her father. Despite the protests of the princess, George remounted his horse, readied his lance, and waited for the dragon's arrival.

Within moments, the creature appeared, crawling up out of the water. It walked low to the ground on stubby legs, trailing a long, scaly tail behind it. The smell of death and decay rolled over George as the monster opened its fanged mouth and roared. It gazed at George with pure malice in its large, yellow eyes. His horse shied away, but George kept it from bolting. Then, kicking the warhorse in the flanks, he charged straight toward the dragon. The princess screamed as the two combatants came together. George ducked to one side as the dragon snapped its jaws at his legs, then he drove his lance into the monster's long snout, piercing it from top to bottom, and pinning its mouth shut. George leapt down from his horse, and climbed onto the monster's back. Grabbing hold of the lance, he held down the dragon's head to keep it from thrashing from side to side. Then he shouted to the princess, telling her to take off her long girdle and tie it around the dragon's neck. When the princess had done this, the dragon became calm, and George stepped off its back.

George then led the way to the gates of the town, followed by the princess, leading the dragon by her girdle. The townsfolk refused to open the gates in fear of the dragon, but George proclaimed that he would kill the dragon if they would convert to Christianity. The people agreed, so George drew his sword and beheaded the creature with one, clean stroke. Later that day, the whole town was baptized in the river, which once again flowed clear.

After the ceremony, the king offered George any reward he wished, including his daughter's hand in marriage. George turned down all his offers, and asked only that the king build a church, and remember the Lord in all things. Then George departed to complete his mission for Tribune Constantine.

(Opposite) *The Historical St. George.* This artwork is an attempt to depict a "historical" encounter between St. George and the dragon. St. George is shown fighting in a manner appropriate to a Roman cavalryman of the 3rd or 4th century. The "dragon" is a very large crocodile.

In all, it took nearly five years for George to complete his task and return to Nicomedia, but the Empire had changed greatly while he had been gone. A group of Christians had been accused of subverting the Empire and been executed. The Praetorian Guard had burned down the Cathedral of Nicomedia, and Christianity had been outlawed, at the insistence of Diocletian's general, and Constantine's rival, Galerius. Enraged by what he found, George went to the temple of Bacchus and threw down the statue of the Roman god, smashing it to pieces. He did the same at a temple of Hercules, and probably would have continued his rampage had not the Praetorian Guard wrestled him to the ground and thrown him in prison.

Painting of St. George entitled *Eternal Victory* by Frank O. Salisbury. This painting was completed and displayed in Britain during World War II to symbolize the triumph of truth and justice over Hitler. (Peter Nahum at The Leicester Galleries, London / Bridgeman Art Library)

Even held in a dark, dank prison, George refused to renounce his Christianity, and so the Romans tortured him repeatedly. They made him walk in shoes of iron spikes. They hung him on a wheel with metal hooks that pierced his flesh. They burned him with torches and scourged him with whips. For three weeks the torturers delighted in their cruelty, but at the end of each week, when George lay alone in his cell, the Archangel Michael came down from heaven to heal George of his wounds and renewed his faith. When the people of Rome heard the stories of George's courage and his miraculous healing, more and more of them secretly turned to Christianity.

Emperor Diocletian's man Galerius, enraged at the failure of his torturers, instead turned to dark magic, and sent a magician named Athanasius to convert or kill George. Athanasius prepared a dark, poisonous brew, filled with serpent's venom, that he knew would either kill George, or turn him into his mindless zombie slave. When George drank the evil mixture, however, it had no effect upon him. Stunned, Athanasius fell to his knees and admitted the power of the Lord.

Saint George and the Dragon by Raphael.

As more and more Romans began to turn from the old ways, Emperor Diocletian offered George his freedom if he would leave the Empire, never to return. George refused, knowing he had one last task to perform for the Lord. Consequently, Diocletian ordered George beheaded in a public execution. So, on 23 April 303 CE, the Romans led George to a public square in Nicomedia, read the Emperor's order of execution, and struck off his head.

The death of George, soon to be called St. George, was a spark that ignited a change of heart in many Romans. One man who was particularly struck by the tragedy was Tribune Constantine, who, when he became Emperor three years later, would convert the whole Empire to Christianity.

છ૭•છ૭•છ૭•છ૭•છ૭•છ૭

According to popular mythology, the legend of St. George was brought to England from the Holy Land by the Crusaders. This is, however, untrue. The story of St. George's martyrdom spread slowly across the whole of the Christianized world during the fourth century, through both written accounts and the dispersal of the saint's numerous relics. He was canonized as a saint in 494 CE. His first appearance in an English source comes from 679 CE, when the

Saint George and the Dragon by Tintoretto.

(Opposite) St. George as depicted in a German World War I propaganda poster.

Abbot of Iona wrote a tale concerning a traveler who called upon St. George for protection, a story that is repeated by the Venerable Bede. The first full account of St. George's martyrdom in English was Aelfric's *Passion of Saint George*, written in the first half of the eleventh century. However, none of the accounts mentioned above contain a dragon, nor do any of the earliest versions of the St. George story.

The first associations of a dragon with St. George probably come from the Greek Church, where early icons depicted St. George trampling the Dragon of the Apocalypse, representing the saint's triumph over evil. This association seems to have spread out from Greece in the ninth and tenth centuries, and was soon seen in imagery all over Europe. The first written account of the battle between St. George and the dragon comes from the twelfth century. In that story, George subdues the dragon with the sign of the cross, a familiar motif seen in many saint-versus-dragon legends.

The turning point for the story of St. George and the dragon came in the year 1260, when the Italian Jacobus de Voragine compiled a large collection of saints's lives into a work now known as *The Golden Legend*. This work became one of the most popular books of its day, and hundreds of copies have survived to the present. In 1483, England's first book printer, William Caxton, translated *The Golden Legend* into English, and it became a popular work among the educated and well-to-do.

While *The Golden Legend* only tells a brief version of the story of St. George and the dragon, it contains all of the classic aspects that have become associated with the tale: the citizens feeding their children to the dragon, George saving the princess, and the binding of the dragon with a girdle. It is from *The Golden Legend* that the modern story of St. George has developed.

E. Kaempffer

THE HISTORICAL ST. GEORGE

Despite the enduring popularity of the St. George legend, almost every aspect of the story is open to debate and speculation. Indeed, any search for the "true historical St. George" is something of a fool's errand as even the earliest versions of his life are full of contradictions. In fact, as early as 494 CE, Pope Gelasius I, while canonizing George, warned that the story of St. George should be treated with "extreme circumspection."

St. George is sometimes said to be from Cappadocia in modern Turkey, but this may result from confusion with another historical figure named "George of Cappadocia," a far from saintly man. Just as likely, St. George came from Palestine, where the towns of Joppa and Diospolis both claim the honor. His parentage is unknown, though many possibilities are given in the various accounts. Even his position as a Roman soldier or officer cannot be convincingly confirmed. All that can truly be said is that there was probably a man named George, who lived somewhere in the Middle-East or North Africa in the third century CE who was martyred for his faith by the Romans.

Since the earliest days of the legend, many countries have tried to claim the saint as their own. At various times St. George has been identified as the patron saint of Portugal, Germany, Armenia, Hungary and Lithuania, as well as numerous cities from as far and wide as Ferrara, Antioch, Braganza and Bellay. Yet no location seems to have staked its claim harder than England. In the centuries since *The Golden Legend*, many versions of the St. George story have been written in English, and in each one, George seems to become a little more, well, English.

Around 1580, Richard Johnson wrote *The Famous Historie of the Seaven Champions of Christendom*. In this popular version of the tale, St. George is a native of Coventry who journeys to Egypt, fights a dragon and marries the princess. He then brings his bride back to England, where they have a long life together, before George fights a second dragon, which results in the death of both combatants (reminiscent of Beowulf). In this version, St. George is also the father of another noted dragonslayer, Guy of Warwick, who will be discussed later.

While the story of St. George was gaining wide popular appeal among the English populace, it was also being used more and more frequently by the royalty. The first monarch to have been really interested in the story of St. George was Edward III, and there is more than one medieval manuscript in existence that shows Edward III and St. George standing together. In the mid-1340s, Edward III established the Order of the Garter, one of the most famous English knightly orders, and designated the chapel of St. George at Windsor as its focal point. In 1349 the first formal celebration of St. George's Day took place in the chapel.

Saint George and the Dragon by Santi Raffaelli. (Lebrecht Music and Arts Photo Library / Alamy)

From then until today, St. George has been frequently and increasingly used by the English as a symbol of national identity. Even during the Reformation of Henry VIII, when the king banned nearly all religious holidays, St. George's Day was given an exemption. Now, even as religion plays a diminishing role in the lives of most English people, it appears that the celebration of St. George's Day will continue for many, many years to come.

Pope Sylvester I

Not long after Constantine became the Emperor of Rome, a great dragon took up residence in a deep pit on the edge of the city. From this pit, the creature's foul, poisonous breath would drift up and roll across the city. Nearly three hundred people a day suffered sickness and death from the foul fumes, and they cried out to the Emperor for help and protection.

Pope St. Sylvester's Miracle, a fresco painted on the wall of the San Silvestro Chapel around 1337. (Mandadori Electa / The Bridgeman Art Library)

(Opposite) *The Redcrosse Knight*. In 1590 the English poet, Edmund Spenser, released the first part of his epic poem, *The Faerie Queene*. The hero of book one is The Redcrosse Knight, who is later revealed to be St. George. In the poem, St. George kills a dragon after an epic battle. This artwork illustrates this battle, one of the last major fights between a hero and a dragon in English literature before the works of J. R. R. Tolkien.

Unsure how to deal with the dragon, Constantine summoned Pope Sylvester and asked his advice. The Pope replied that he would pray on the matter, and that God would show him the way to defeat the creature.

That night, Sylvester prayed to God and to all the saints who had gone before him for guidance. Then St. Peter, the first pope, appeared to him. Peter taught Sylvester a prayer to tame the dragon, and gave to Sylvester a silver thread to bind its mouth.

As the sun rose the following morning, Sylvester went alone to the great pit. Despite the poisonous fumes that boiled up around the pit, he walked safely to the edge of the hole. There he found a great staircase leading down. Lighting a pair of lanterns, he descended into the darkness. The staircase spiraled around the edge of the hole, running downward for one hundred and fifty steps, and, at the bottom, Sylvester found the dragon curled up amidst the bones of its many victims.

As Sylvester approached, it reared up and gazed down at the pope with baleful eyes.

Sylvester put down his lanterns, raised up his hands, and spoke:

Our Lord Jesus Christ which was born of the Virgin Mary, crucified, buried and arose, and now sitteth on the right side of the Father, this is he that shall come to deem and judge the living and the dead, I commend thee Sathanas [Satan] that thou abide him in this place till he comes.

St. Crantock (or Carantoc) as depicted in stained glass from Crantock Church in Cornwall. (Photographed by S. Tyson / Dan Mersey)

Then Sylvester took the silver thread and bound shut the dragon's mouth, so that its breath could not escape. Sylvester returned to the surface, bringing the dragon with him to show everyone what had been done. The people of Rome rejoiced to be delivered from the creature, and many asked to be baptized on the spot.

ↂ•ↂ•ↂ•ↂ•ↂ•ↂ

Sylvester served as the pope from 314 to 335 CE. Although little can be said for certain about him, he reigned during a time of great growth and expansion for the Catholic Church. It was during his time that many great churches were built in Rome, including the first St. Peter's Basilica. He also approved the decisions of the Council of Nicaea, the first great ecumenical council that codified a lot of early church doctrine.

The story of Sylvester and the dragon comes from *The Golden Legend*, where it serves as an addendum to a longer and more famous story about the pope and Constantine. In this tale, God strikes Constantine with leprosy because of his persecution of Christians. When Constantine goes to his physicians, they say the disease can only be cured by bathing in the blood of three thousand children. The Emperor has his soldiers gather the children, but when he hears the wailing of their mothers, he decides not to kill them. Because of this, God sends him a message to go to Sylvester and be baptized. Upon his baptism, Constantine is cured.

The baptism story, like many other stories about Sylvester, was probably written in an effort to establish the authority of the church over that of secular rulers, and it is certainly possible to see the dragon story in this light. However, regardless of why the dragon story was written, it follows a very classic formula for saint-versus-dragon stories. Sylvester overcomes the dragon with the power of prayer and then binds it with something frail. What is somewhat unusual about the tale is that the final fate of the dragon is not stated. In almost all other stories of this type, including St. George above and St. Carantoc below, the dragon is led back to the people it menaced and then either killed or banished. Sylvester's dragon, on the other hand, is brought up from the pit, and then the story just ends.

St. Carantoc and King Arthur

King Arthur paused atop the hill and looked back at the long column of men and horses that followed behind. For three weeks, they had hunted along the Cornish coast, following a trail of mutilated cattle and burning villages, but still had failed to find the dragon responsible. The only break in their monotonous search had been the discovery last week of a strange wooden table, washed up on the shore. The table was decorated with intricate carvings of men and beasts, and though it had apparently drifted on the ocean tides, it had suffered no damage. That night, they had tried to use the table for their supper, but any dish placed upon its surface was immediately cast upon the ground by some mysterious magical force. So they gave up and packed the table away, and it now traveled in one of the wagons in the rear.

When Arthur turned back around, he saw an old man struggling up the other side of the hill. He carried a gnarled wooden stick and wore simple robes and a white stole, embroidered with a golden cross around his shoulders.

"Father," said the king, as the man came closer, "by what name do you travel? And what brings you to this lonely place?"

The old man smiled. "I am called Carantoc, and I suspect that I am here for the same reason as you. I am hunting."

At this, Arthur drew back. "Not hunting for the dragon, surely?"

"Dragon?" replied Carantoc. "No. Dragons are easy to find. I'm hunting for my altar. I tossed it into the sea many months ago and have been searching for it ever since. Wherever it comes ashore, I shall build a church."

St. Clément of Metz, the first bishop of Metz, fighting with the dragon Graoully. This stained glass window was designed by Hermann de Munster in the 14th century and can be seen in the Cathedral of Metz in France.

SAINTLY DRAGONSLAYERS

St. Beatus of Lungern
(The Apostle of Switzerland)

Born in either Scotland or Ireland in the first century, Beatus was ordained as a priest in Rome by St. Peter. He then traveled to Switzerland to preach and baptize. Late in his life, Beatus traveled into the mountains above Lake Thun, where he battled a dragon. Beatus would live out the rest of his life as a hermit in the dragon's cave.

St. Clement of Metz

Sent out by St. Peter in the earliest days of the Church, St. Clement traveled to Metz, where he found the local population being held prisoner by a dragon. This dragon, known as the Graoully, had taken up residence in the ruins of the Roman amphitheatre, along with an army of lesser serpents. Using the sign of the cross, Clement tamed the Graoully and his serpents and banished them from the world of men and animals.

St. Murrough O'Heany

Soon after the death of St. Patrick, a great dragon called Lig-na-Paiste terrorized the Roe Valley in Ireland, and the people called upon Murrough to save them. After praying for nine days, Murrough went to the dragon

"You say dragons are easy prey, but I would gladly trade knowledge of your altar to see the dragon that plagues this land."

"Indeed?" said Carantoc. "Well, wait here my king and you shall see." Carantoc turned and walked back down the hill. Then he knelt down in prayer by a long stretch of marshy ground.

A few moments later, the ground rumbled, and Arthur stared in amazement as a winged dragon burst from the earth. It gave a pathetic cry from its fanged mouth, like a calf calling to its mother, and came running over to the holy man. There it laid its head down by the old man's feet. Carantoc stood up, removed his stole, and wrapped it gently around the dragon's neck. Then, leading the dragon behind him, Carantoc walked back up the hill to where King Arthur stood. Arthur reached for his sword, but Carantoc laid a gentle hand upon his.

"You asked to see the dragon and you have done so. There is no need for swords. I shall banish it from this place, never to return."

King Arthur nodded. "And I shall bring you your altar, and then I will take you to the place where my men found it."

Carantoc banished the dragon, and Arthur kept his promise. He took St. Carantoc to the spot where they had found the altar. Then the king and his men helped the holy man build his church.

ↄ·ↄ·ↄ·ↄ·ↄ·ↄ

St. Carantoc, whose name is also spelled Crantock, Carannog, Cairnech, or Carantocus, was a sixth century saint born in either Wales or Cornwall. What little is known about his life comes from a fantastical biography, and challenged him to a contest. If Paiste would allow Murrough to place three rods upon his back, the dragon could then try to eat him. The dragon agreed, but when Murrough placed the rods across his back, they immediately grew down into the ground, pinning Paiste to the earth. Murrough then banished the dragon until Judgement Day, into the waters of Lough Foyle, where, it is said, he still struggles against his bonds. Paiste was the last serpent in Ireland.

St. Theodore Tyro

A contemporary of St. George, Theodore also served as a cavalryman in the Roman Army. While stationed near his hometown of Amasea in Turkey, he heard tell of a fire-breathing dragon attacking the people nearby. He found the dragon near an abandoned village and killed it with a spear thrust to the head. Theodore was later martyred for his Christian faith, which he had kept secret for most of his life.

The Blessed Ammon

According to Rufinus in his *Historia Monachorum in Aegypto*, the blessed Ammon encountered a giant dragon with poisonous breath in the midst of the Egyptian desert. Ammon called upon the power of God to strike down the charging dragon, and the dragon immediately vomited up his life and burst with a loud crack. Ammon is thought to have been the first hermit to found a Monastery.

St. Bernard of Menthon

Born in the early tenth century, St. Bernard ran away from his rich family to become a priest in the Benedictine order. From then on, he devoted his life to the conversion of the people living in the Alps. In one story, while traveling in the Alps, St. Bernard and his followers came across a brigand who was using a dragon to terrorize the local populace. Bernard went up to the dragon and threw his stole across it. The middle part of the stole miraculously turned into chains that wrapped around the dragon's neck. Thus chained, Bernard's followers were able to dispatch the beast.

St. Magnus

Probably the most prolific of all holy dragonslayers, St. Magnus was born around the year 700. Later that century, Magnus would go on a dragonslaying tour around southern Germany. He defeated his first dragon, a monster named Boas, near the city of Kempten, bashing in its head with a staff. In the valley of Rosshaupten he faced another dragon. This one he killed by tossing pitch and resin into its mouth, causing it to explode. Finally, at the village of Ronsberg, St. Magnus faced off against three dragons. These he defeated by unleashing a pack of trained bears that hunted them down and tore them to shreds.

Though it is hard to believe, these are just the best known of the many dragons that St. Magnus is said to have killed or banished during his lifetime, and his total may reach as high as eighteen!

St. Bernard and the dragon.

Saint Magnus by Andreas Brugger. (INTERFOTO / Alamy)

preserved in a twelfth century manuscript. At the time he lived, the Celtic Church was mostly disconnected from the Roman Catholic Church, and it is only in later generations, with the reintegration of the two, that the lives of the early Celtic saints became part of the Catholic tradition.

While the story of St. Carantoc and the dragon still survives as a folktale in parts of Cornwall, and a church still stands on the supposed site that his altar washed ashore, it is the association with King Arthur that has likely preserved it. Because Arthur remains such a popular legend, any early work which contains him is closely studied, especially those stories that, like St. Carantoc's, appear independent of the later British traditions that mostly stem from the works of Geoffery of Monmouth.

Arthur's role in this story is very similar to that of Constantine in the story of St. Sylvester. Again, we have a powerful secular ruler whose lands are under threat by a dragon, but who proves powerless to stop it. St. Carantoc then comes along to demonstrate the supremacy of the power of the Church. Also like the story of St. Sylvester and that of St. George, the defeated dragon is bound with something frail and taken captive. In the story of St. George the dragon is killed, while in the story of St. Sylvester the dragon's fate isn't stated. In the story of Carantoc, however, the saint stops anyone from killing the dragon, perhaps arguing that only God should be the arbiter of life and death, even in the case of dragons.

MEDIEVAL DRAGONSLAYERS

As Europe passed from the Dark Ages into the Medieval period, it witnessed the development of a new type of dragonslayer story, built upon, but distinct from, the earlier traditions. During this time, dragons lost most of their mythic power, and people came to view them less and less as embodiments of satanic evil, or avatars of chaos. Instead, dragons became just monsters. Ferocious monsters that possessed deadly fangs, impenetrable armor, and even poisonous or fiery breath, it is true, but still just mortal creatures. No longer did it require the power of God, or even a hero of epic proportions, to slay a dragon. During this time, brave knights and even wily peasants could potentially best a dragon.

These new dragonslayers were folk heroes, and, like most folktales, their stories grew out of the attempt by a local population to explain the world around them. In some cases, dragon stories explained geographic features, such as the knuckerholes in Sussex. These watery caves or sinkholes were said

Woodcut of a Viking knight slaying a dragon. Photograph by Wolfgang Sauber.

to have once contained knuckers (a term for water-dragons, derived from the Old English). Dragonslayer stories also became popular explanations for the use of a dragon, or more commonly a wyvern (a two-legged dragon), in the heraldry of many families. These stories had the bonus for the families in question of giving them a heroic, dragonslaying ancestor. In a similar vein, many of the stories probably developed to explain misunderstood dragon iconography left over from previous ages. In earlier times dragons were often used as visual symbols of evil; however, later generations often didn't remember or understand what these depictions meant, and so they invented local stories to explain them.

Like all attempts to classify a diverse body of narrative traditions, there are numerous exceptions to the explanations above. Also, it would be incorrect to view the medieval dragonslayer tradition in isolation. In many places, the tradition of the Holy Dragonslayers continued to develop and expand at the same time. Also, it is during this time that most of the older Norse traditions were first written down. What is clear, however, is that the medieval period was the last great age in which most of the population actually believed in dragons and in the heroic stories of their slayers. In the later Middle Ages, the legends of the dragonslayers gave way to fictional romances and fairy tales. Contained below are four of the most famous examples of medieval dragonslayer stories, each of which likely developed for a different reason.

John Lambton and the Lambton Worm

Back in the quiet years before the war between king and parliament, the young John Lambton lived a life of privileged idleness. Heir to the vast Lambton estates, John was a headstrong boy, reckless and rebellious, who cared little for the authority of his parents or of the Church. One Sunday, while good men honored the day of the Lord, John went fishing in the River Wear. He wasted the day, lying on the bank, catching nothing but the occasional nap. Then, as the sun began its decline, he got a nibble on his line. Grabbing his pole, he pulled in his catch and discovered a hideous worm dangling from the hook. The creature was three feet long and had a row of holes running back from its head on either side of his body. At first John thought to take the creature home with him, but on his walk back to the manor house, he changed his mind and tossed the creature in a well.

The years passed, and John matured. He left the idle youth behind and became an honest, hard-working man. However, he lamented the wasted years when he'd caused so much mischief, and vowed that he would make amends. Against the wishes of his father, John took up the sword and left England to fight for the Lord God in distant lands. Eventually, he joined with the Knights of Rhodes and fought with them in many battles. In later years, he would speak very little of this time, saying only that he had done his duty.

Meanwhile, back at the Lambton estates, a great horror had struck the land. The worm, which John had carelessly thrown in a well so many years before, had grown to monstrous proportions. The creature could swallow a sheep whole, and would tear the throats from horses and cattle. Worse still, it crawled through the land, tainting everything with its poisoned breath, so that crops failed to grow and game animals fled to other regions. Many men went to fight the hideous beast, but their swords and spears could not penetrate the dragon's scales. A few were lucky to escape with their lives; most were crushed to death in the dragon's coils.

So the Lambton lands emptied, until only the family and a few loyal retainers remained. John's father, that once proud man, aged two years for

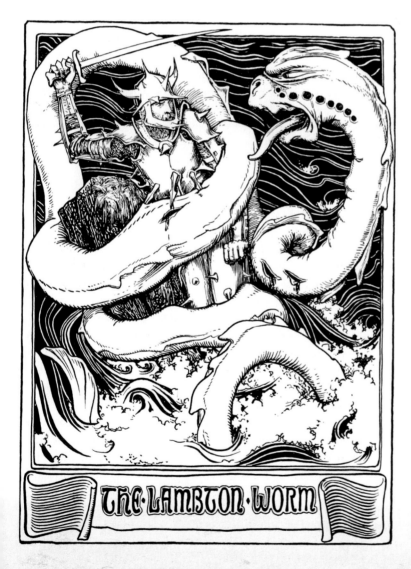

THE·LAMBTON·WORM

John Lambton battles the Lambton Worm.

BRITISH DRAGONSLAYERS

Despite its small size, Britain contains a huge number and variety of dragon and dragonslayer stories. Contained below are a few of the most famous and interesting.

Piers Shonks

The wily Piers Shonks not only slew a dragon, but he outwitted the devil as well. During his time as the Lord of Pelham, a dragon took up residence in the tangled roots of an ancient Yew tree near the village of Brent Pelham. Determined to rid his land of this menace, Piers had a special suit of spiked armor forged. Then, accompanied by his three best hounds, he set off with sword and lance to face the dragon. The fight proved swift and bloody; while the hounds snapped at the dragon's legs, Piers drove his lance down the monster's throat, killing it. However, as soon as it died, the devil appeared. The dragon had been one of his favorites. He cursed Piers and declared that he would claim his soul after his death, whether he was buried in the church or outside of it.

Years later, as Piers lay on his deathbed, he sent for a servant and explained his last wishes. When Piers died, they buried his body in the walls of the church at Brent Pelham. Since his body lay neither inside the church nor outside of it, the devil was cheated of his prize.

Sir Guy of Warwick

A legendary English knight, popular in the medieval Romances of the thirteenth century, and still popular in books of the seventeenth century, Sir Guy is credited with the slaying of multiple dragons. His most famous dragon story took place in Longwitton, near three holy wells. During his first fight with the dragon, Sir Guy inflicted many wounds, but watched in amazement as they healed almost instantly. Sir Guy was badly beaten in the fight and barely escaped with his life. After healing up, he returned to fight the dragon a second time. Again he struck several blows that healed instantly, but this time he noticed that the dragon always kept its tail down one of the wells. Although Sir Guy was forced to retreat

again, he would return a third time, with a new plan. Faking a retreat during the third fight, Sir Guy managed to get between the dragon and the wells. Thereafter, as Sir Guy struck blows, the wounds did not heal, and eventually he killed the dragon.

Fulk Fitzwarren

There is an Iron Age fort near the village of Norton Fitzwarren in Somerset. According to local legend, the Romans had slaughtered native Britons on the site, and somehow the death and rotting corpses eventually created a dragon through spontaneous generation. This dragon attacked the local populace from its perch on the hilltop fort, until a wandering knight named Fulk Fitzwarren dispatched it in a fight.

John Conyers

During the reign of Richard I, John Conyers of Sockburn donned spiked armor and slew a dragon that was terrorizing the area. As a reward, the king awarded him the Manor of Sockburn. For hundreds of years afterwards, it was traditional for the current Lord of Sockburn Manor to go and greet any new Bishop of Durham. At this meeting, the lord would present the bishop with the 'Conyers Falchion', the sword that had been used to slay the dragon. The bishop would take the sword and immediately return it, wishing health upon the lord. Although this tradition has lapsed in modern times, the falchion itself can still be viewed in the treasury of Durham Cathedral.

Teárlach Sgiobair

A variation of the spiked armor idea was used by Teárlach Sgiobair (Charles the Skipper) in his battle with the dragon of Beinn a' Bheithir in the Highlands. This dragon had taken up residence in a cave on a cliff side that overlooked a road by the ocean. From this high perch, it would leap down to attack unwary travelers. For years, no one dared face the monster until Teárlach Sgiobair came along. An experienced seaman, Teárlach guided his boat until it sat just off the Argyll shore, below the lair of the dragon. He then constructed a pontoon bridge built of barrels connecting the boat to the land. Each of the barrels he covered in sharpened spikes. Teárlach then made a fire on his boat and began to roast meat. When the dragon smelled the cooked meat, it leapt down from its cave and charged across the spiked bridge, cutting itself to ribbons. It died before it ever reached the boat. As it turns out, this dragon had left behind some hatchlings when it was killed. Luckily a farmer found the hatchlings hiding in a haystack and burned it and them.

Seigneur de Hambye

While Seigneur de Hambye is not technically a "British Dragonslayer," the story itself comes from the Channel Island of Jersey. In this tale, Seigneur de Hambye from Normandy traveled to Jersey to free the population from the terror of a dragon. After a long and brutal fight, the knight defeated the monster by cutting off its head. Wounded and exhausted, Seigneur de Hambye sat down to rest and was murdered by his ambitious squire. The squire then cut out the dragon's tongue, which he took back to Normandy. Claiming he had killed the dragon, the squire married his master's widow and took control of his estates. However, the squire talked in his sleep, and, one night, his new wife heard his confession and had him arrested. The squire eventually admitted his guilt, while awake, and was executed.

every one, doubly plagued by the dragon and the conviction that his son had died in some distant battle. He withdrew into his crumbling manor house, spending his days in brooding isolation.

Seven years to the day that John Lambton had left England, he returned to her shores. Battle-scarred and weary, he longed to see his home and to once again sit by the fire with his father to talk away the cold and rainy nights. But as John rode towards his family home, his heart sank. The once green fields were barren and dead, and the trees had withered. No birds flew in the sky; no hares scampered from the hedges. When he reached the house of his youth, he frowned at the decaying walls and empty, lifeless windows. Inside, he found his father, sitting alone in his study, staring blankly at an empty fireplace. The old man looked up, and John's heart nearly broke to see his father's tearful smile.

For the next few days, John worked tirelessly to organize what remained of the household. At the same time, he learned all he could of the dragon that so plagued his father's lands. His many years as a soldier had taught him well; he knew the foolishness of charging headfirst into battle against an unknown enemy. When he had learned all he could from the household, he rode out alone one night, to seek the old witch-woman who used to live in the marshes on the edge of the Lambton lands.

He found the hag in her old straw hut, casting unwholesome items into an old iron caldron. She smiled a broken-toothed smile as John Lambton approached, and began to speak before he even asked a question.

"So you've finally come about your worm," spoke the hag. "Yes, it is your worm. The creature you carelessly tossed in a well so many years ago. It grew!

The coat of arms of the German town of Heide. It is just one example of the numerous cities and towns in Europe that feature dragons and/or dragonslayers in their official coat of arms.

It grew! Now you want to know how to kill it? Well I will tell you. No hand of man is strong enough to pierce those scales with sword or spear. You must build a new suit of armor, one covered in blades. Then stand in the river and let the dragon come to you. It will cut itself on the blades, and then you may strike. You must throw its pieces into the river, lest they grow together again. A price? Of course there is a price. After you have killed the worm, you must kill the next living creature you encounter. That is the price. If you do not pay this price, no Lambton will die peacefully in bed for nine generations."

So John returned home with the witch-woman's words lingering in his ears. The next morning he pulled out the armor he'd worn on campaign. Then he gathered all of the old knives and spears from the house's armory. With patience and care, he welded the blades and spearheads onto his armor so that the metal spikes pointed in every direction. When he had finished, he told his father what he intended to do. His father pleaded with him not to face the dragon, but John would not be dissuaded. He told his father that once he had killed the worm, he would blow on his horn. Then his father must release his old hound. It was the old hound who must pay the witch-woman's price.

On a dreary autumn morning, John set out towards the River Wear. By the river, he found a ford where the worm liked to cross the fast-flowing waters. John donned his suit of spiked armor and stood on a rock in the middle of the Wear. Then he waited. In those hours, he remained sharp-eyed and alert, in sharp contrast to the lazy day so many years before when he had caught the worm. Eventually, he heard the creature approach, crawling through the dead shrubs by the riverside, and John recognized it by the line of holes running along its sides. It gave a poisonous hiss, then plunged into the water.

John watched its shadowy form approach from under the water, then flinched back as it burst forth and coiled itself around him. The coils constricted, forcing the air from John's lungs. However, the strength of the dragon's coils was also its undoing. The beast wound itself so tight that the blades on the armor cut through its scales, opening up numerous wounds. Fighting for air, John took his sword and hacked at those wounds, severing numerous chunks from the worm. These chunks fell into the river and were washed away by the current.

Drenched in the dragon's blood, and still struggling to breathe, John drove his sword through a gaping wound, up into the dragon's brain. Suddenly the coils loosened, and what remained of the worm fell away, sliding into the water to be borne away by the river. John struggled to shore, took his horn in his bloody hand, and blew a victorious blast.

(Opposite) *The Lambton Worm.* By the medieval period, most European dragons were depicted as having four limbs; however, in most English folktales, dragons continued to appear as giant serpents.

Back at the manor house, John's father heard the horn. He released the hound, but was so overcome by relief at his son's victory that he too ran to greet his son. John waited by the riverside, slowly removing his bloody, spiked armor. He glanced up and saw, appearing on the brow of a low hill, not the hound he had expected, but his father. His hand trembled. A moment later, the hound came running up, and, with a heavy heart, John took his sword and pierced the faithful dog through the heart, killing it swiftly and without suffering. Silently he prayed that the price was paid, but knew in his heart that it was not.

Father and son had a tearful reunion on the riverbank, and John decided that he would never tell his father that he had seen him first. The old man would die a few years later, happily unaware of the curse that now lay upon his family.

ↄ•ↄ•ↄ•ↄ•ↄ•ↄ

After the legend of St. George, the Lambton Worm is probably Britain's best-known dragonslayer legend. It is impossible to say exactly when the story developed; for many centuries it was preserved as an oral folktale and a popular folk song, and many versions of both can still be found.

As a dragonslaying story, it contains a mix of common and unique elements. For reasons that are not clear, the idea of using spiked armor to defeat a dragon is a motif that occurs frequently in British folktales. Also, the idea that a dragon can reattach its severed parts occurs in several British stories. On the other hand, two elements of the story are nearly unique. The first is the idea that the hero, the dragonslayer himself, is the cause of the dragon plague in the first place. Perhaps this is related to the Christian idea of penance; the sinner must do his best to undo the sin. The other oddity is the attachment to the story of the curse. In all likelihood, this part of the story was added at a much later date. According to the legend, the curse would affect the Lambton family for nine generations. It is true that two Lambtons were killed in the English Civil War, and their immediate predecessor drowned. One hundred and twenty years later, another died in a carriage accident. Probably, the curse was added to the story in order to explain these deaths.

Dieudonné de Gozon, Draconis Extinctor

It was in the middle years of the fourteenth century, while Grand Master Hélion de Villeneuve led the Knights of St. John, that a dragon came to the island of Rhodes. Perhaps it flew in from some distant land, or maybe it swam across the sea from Africa. Either way, it made its home in a cave about two miles from the city of Rhodes, at a place now called Malpasso. From its lair, the dragon would venture out to feast upon sheep and the occasional passing traveler and pilgrim.

When word of the attacks reached the Knights, many volunteered to ride out and face the dragon alone, as chivalry demanded, and the Grand Master selected his strongest and bravest knight. This knight set out the next day to face the dragon, but he never returned. When several days had passed without word, a second knight was selected. He too rode out with a sharp sword and gleaming armor, never to return. Grieved by the loss of two of his bravest knights, Grand Master de Villeneuve forbade anyone else from facing the dragon. Shepherds must move their sheep, and travelers would have to take a different road. The Knights of St. John could not defeat the beast.

There was one among the Knights, however, who did not agree with the Grand Master's decision, a young, headstrong man named Dieudonné de Gozon. Soon after the death of the brave knights, Dieudonné received leave to visit his home in France. There, in the house of his father, Dieudonné constructed a life-sized model of the dragon. It was the size of a horse, with the head of a snake, and ears like a donkey. It had four legs, short like a crocodile's, and small wings resembling a bat. He gave it a skin of canvas and stuffed the creature with straw.

For the next several weeks, Dieudonné trained with his horse and dogs to fight the dragon. The horse he trained to approach the creature without shying. He taught the dogs to attack the creature's legs and underside, while he practiced with his lance to spear it from horseback. When, finally, the young knight felt confident, he left his home with his dogs and quietly sailed back to the island of Rhodes. He avoided the city and the Knights of his order, and instead put in at an isolated cove. From there, he rode via a back way to the cave of the dragon.

As Dieudonné approached the cave, he was nearly overcome by the rotten stench. He could see dark bloodstains on the ground, and pieces of dented armor lying about. His dogs growled as they too scented something foul in the air. Then the dragon appeared, a malevolent serpent, just like the one Dieudonné had constructed to train his animals. It flapped its wings and gave a shrieking cry.

Dieudonné whistled and his dogs sprang forward. They leapt at the dragon's short legs, latching on with their powerful jaws. The dragon swatted one dog aside, disemboweling it with its razor-sharp talons. It snatched up another with a coil of its serpent's tail and broke its back upon the ground. Yet still the remaining dogs held on, tugging the dragon off balance.

Many people have theorized that the dragon of Rhodes was in fact a crocodile, as depicted in this drawing. (Lebrecht Music and Arts Photo Library)

PHORBAS

The island of Rhodes had trouble with dragons long before the time of Dieudonné de Gozon. According to the myths and legends of Ancient Greece, a horde of serpents, including one gigantic dragon-serpent, overran in the island in the distant past. The islanders called upon a hero named Phorbas, who came to Rhodes and slaughtered or drove out all of the serpents. For his deeds he was immortalized as the constellation Ophiuchus.

Dieudonné saw his chance. With the dragon distracted by the dogs, he spurred his horse forward. As the horse's hooves pounded on the hard earth, Dieudonné lowered his lance. The point impacted square on the dragon's head, piercing its skull, driving through its brain, and bursting out of its lower jaw. The dragon died in an instant and collapsed to the ground.

When Dieudonné returned to the preceptory of his order, carrying the dragon's head as proof of his deed, he was greeted as a hero by his fellow knights. Grand Master de Villeneuve, however, was less impressed. He charged Dieudonné with disobeying orders. He stripped him of his habit, of his status as a Knight of St. John, and threw him into the dungeon. There Dieudonné stayed for many days, while the Grand Master's temper cooled. Eventually Hélion de Villeneuve relented. He released Dieudonné from his prison and reinstated him in the order. He also ordered the dragon's head mounted over the main gate of the city as a symbol of the bravery of the Knights of St. John.

Many years later, the Knights of St. John elected Dieudonné as Grand Master of the order, and he led the Knights with honor and distinction. When Dieudonné eventually died in 1353, his gravestone was marked with the words 'Extinctor Draconis'.

❧ ❧ ❧ ❧ ❧ ❧

Outside of the saints, there are few documented historical figures who are also dragonslayers. Although very little is actually known of Dieudonné de Gozon, he appears in the historical record as the Grand Master of the Knights of Saint John, better known as the Knights Hospitaller, from 1346 through 1353, making him either the third of fourth leader of that order.

The first account of his battle with the dragon is found in a pilgrim's tale, written in the early part of the sixteenth century. About seventy years later, G. Bosio wrote a longer version of the story in his *Historia della S. Religione di S. Giovanni* (1594). From there, the story passed into the folklore of the island of Rhodes, until it achieved a new popularity in 1799 thanks to a ballad by Friedrich Schiller entitled *Der Kampf mit dem Drachen* (The Fight with the Dragon).

Another interpretation of Dieudonné de Gozon. (Mary Evans Picture Library / Alamy)

Lord Albrecht Trut

For many weeks, the servants of Lord Albrecht Trut had worked on the new town. They had cleared a large stretch of land, felling many trees and cutting them up into boards. They had laid the first foundation stones for the new tower, and marked out the path of the walls. Then one day, as a group of workmen were passing by a deep ravine, they heard a crow crying out shrilly from below. The men looked over the edge and saw a long and deadly dragon emerge from a cave in the wall of the ravine. Terrified, the men ran back to Lord Albrecht and told them what they had seen.

At first Albrecht refused to believe his men. There hadn't been any dragons in the area for generations. Still, something had frightened the workers, so he agreed to take a look. The men led Albrecht back to the ravine. Although the dragon wasn't visible, Albrecht saw its tracks in the dirt around the cave and the old bones of many of its past meals. The young lord immediately came up with a plan.

He ordered his men to run back to the construction site and bring back ropes, chains and wood. Also, he told them to bring the heavy iron gate they planned to use for the town walls and a sheep they could use as bait. The men hurried off and before long had returned with everything their lord had requested. Having assembled everything he needed, Albrecht put his plan into action.

He had his men fashion the ropes and chains into a heavy net. When this was done, they took a rope and lowered the sheep down onto the ground in front of the dragon's cave, with the heavy net dangling a few yards above it. When the loathsome dragon came out of his cave and attacked the poor sheep, Albrecht's men dropped the net, entangling the dragon in its heavy web. The dragon roared in anger and thrashed about, snapping its powerful jaws at the netting. Albrecht knew the net would not hold the creature forever, so he launched the second part of his plan.

The Trutnov dragon clinging to the side of a building. (Al Pulford Photography)

Under his orders, Albrecht's men had built a crane at the top of the ravine. Then they took the iron gate and loaded it up with heavy rocks. Using their crane, they slowly lowered the gate down on top of the dragon, pinning it to the earth under the vast weight. Still the dragon struggled and threatened to topple the gate off of it.

Finally, Albrecht led a group of volunteers down into the ravine. These brave men built a great fire by the dragon's head and then wafted the smoke into its face. In this way, they choked the dragon to death.

Satisfied that the creature was dead, Albrecht ordered his men to skin the creature. For many years, the stuffed dragon skin hung by the gates of the newly built town of Trutnov.

ↄ⋅ↄ⋅ↄ⋅ↄ⋅ↄ⋅ↄ

THE WAWEL DRAGON

One of the most famous dragons in European history, the Wawel Dragon lived at the base of Wawel Hill in what is now the city of Krakow. While all the stories of the Wawel Dragon agree that the beast was slain, they do not always agree on the identity of the dragonslayer. In some stories, King Krakus, the legendary founder of the city, kills the dragon. In other stories, the dragon takes up residence in the city during the reign of Krakus, but the slaying is done by a cobbler's apprentice named Skuba. In this version, Skuba tricks the dragon into eating a lamb stuffed with sulphur. The sulphur makes the dragon so thirsty that it keeps drinking water until it explodes. Skuba is rewarded by marrying the princess.

Regardless of the confusion in the legend, the Wawel Dragon's cave has been turned into a popular tourist attraction, which includes a seven-headed dragon statue that breathes fire at regular intervals.

The Wawel dragon in its cave beneath the city of Krakow.
(Mary Evans Picture Library / Alamy)

The town of Trutnov lies near the northern border of the Czech Republic. The story of its legendary founding is remembered today by a small dragon statue in one of its town parks, a newly developing, annual "dragon festival" and by a metal dragon sculpture that can sometimes be seen clinging to the side of one of the buildings in the town square. According to the legend, the actual dragon skin was eventually given as a gift to the city of Brno, where it still hangs in one of its museums. Of course the citizens of Brno have their own story for the origins of the dragon, a story nearly identical to that of Skuba and the Wawel dragon. Whichever story is believed, the dragon skin hanging in Brno looks decidedly like a crocodile.

Stories such as the Trutnov dragon, the Wawel dragon and the Brno dragon represent a distinct subset of the dragonslayer legend. At one time during the Middle Ages it became a popular trend to have a dragonslaying hero as the legendary town founder, which can also be seen in the aforementioned battle between Jason and the Argonauts and the Ljubljana dragon. Today, many European cities have a dragon as part of their city coat of arms, although determining which came first, the dragon symbol or the dragon story, can often be difficult.

Dobrynya Nikitich and Zmey Gorynych

When Dobrynya was still a young man, his mother gave him four pieces of advice. "Don't ride to the Saracen Mountains. Don't trample baby dragons there. Don't rescue Russian captives, and don't bathe in the Puchai River." Of course, being a valiant young man and a seeker of adventure, that's exactly what he did. Slipping away from home one day, Dobrynya walked up into the craggy peaks of the Saracen Mountains. During his trek, he went out of his way to stamp on any baby dragons that he passed, ensuring that they would never grow up into monsters. He also moved a boulder away from the mouth of a cave, releasing some travelers who had been captured there by a dragon. Finally, Dobrynya made it high into the mountains, near the source of the Puchai River. Tired from his excursions, he decided to take a bath.

While Dobrynya was bathing naked in the river, he felt a rush of wind and looked up to see a mighty three-headed dragon swooping down upon him. In a panic, he swam to the shore and cast about for a weapon. There was nothing there but an old hat of the type worn by Greek pilgrims. He snatched this up as the dragon landed in front of him. As the dragon's middle head reared back, preparing to belch fire, Dobrynya ducked around its heads, leapt upon its back, and used the old hat to clamp its mouth shut. Man and dragon

Dobrynya and Zmey Gorynych by Vasnetsov. In most versions of the tale, Zmey Gorynych has three heads, though occasionally he has twelve. (Global Look / Corbis)

wrestled hard, until they rolled over Dobrynya's clothes that were laid out by the riverside. In that instant, Dobrynya grabbed hold of his knife and put it to the dragon's throat.

"Hold Dobrynya, Nikita's son," said the dragon. "Let us make a pact! You will not come into the Saracen Mountains, nor trample baby dragons, nor rescue Russian captives, nor swim in the Puchai River. In return, I will not fly to Holy Russia. I will not take any Russian captives. I will not carry away any Christian people."

Dobrynya lowered his knife and rolled away from the dragon. "I will hold you to this, Zmey Gorynych. Now go and keep your promises." With that, the dragon beat its mighty wings and leapt into the sky, flying out of sight.

Several years passed. The story of Dobrynya's fight with the dragon had spread around the country. The young man had become a regular at the court of Prince Vladimir, who ruled from his capital at Kiev. Although still not officially honored as a bogatyr, the prince often called upon Dobrynya to serve as his messenger, especially when courtesy or cunning was required.

Then one day, while Vladimir's niece, Zabava, was out walking in the garden, the three-headed dragon, Zmey Gorynych, swooped down from the sky and grabbed the princess in his claws. Before anyone could react, the dragon was gone, flying home to its lair in the mountains. The court was in uproar. Many brave bogatyrs rushed for their arms and clamored for the honor of rescuing the princess, but Prince Vladimir went first to Dobrynya.

"The stories tell that you have bested this dragon before, Dobrynya Nikitich. Go now to the mountains and bring my niece and the dragon's head. If you succeed, you'll be made a bogatyr and greatly rewarded. If you return in cowardice without her, it will be your head that is mounted over the city gate."

So Dobrynya left the court, weighed down with responsibility. He went first to see his mother and told her of his plight. His mother, that wise woman, said he must have a horse. So she gave him the horse, Burko, who had carried both his father and his grandfather on many adventures. She gave him also a whip of seven silks, and told him to use the whip to drive Burko forward. Finally, she gave him a Tartar spear with which to fight. Thus equipped, Dobrynya set off to face the dragon.

He rode up into the Saracen Mountains, and as he rode, the baby dragons attacked Burko's legs. The poor horse trampled them into the dirt, but more and more emerged from the rocks to snap at his fetlocks. When it appeared that Burko might be pulled down by the nasty little creatures, Dobrynya took out his whip and snapped it on the horse's flank. Burko sprang forward, shedding the baby dragons and charging up the slopes.

Near the mountaintop, by the banks of the Puchai River, Dobrynya found the dragon once more.

(Opposite) A modern interpretation of Dobrynya and Zmey Gorynych by Alexander Yatskevich

69

"Hail Dobrynya, Nikita's son," spoke the dragon. "You have failed to keep your promise. You've rode in to the Saracen Mountains, and you've trampled baby dragons. No doubt you've come to rescue Russian captives here."

Dobrynya responded, "Hail Zmey Gorynych. Was it I or you who broke the faith? Did you not swoop down and take the princess, a virtuous Christian woman, and carry her away as your captive? For this treason you must die."

Without further words, the battle was joined. For three long days the brave warrior and the mighty beast battled. The dragon blew fire and bit with its three snake-like heads. Dobrynya dodged and parried, looking for openings to drive in his sharp spear. On and on the battle raged, around the River Puchai, through the rocks of the mountains, and even into the caves underneath it. Both man and monster received and dealt many wounds, until both were covered in bloody cuts. Dobrynya began to despair of ever defeating the dragon, until a voice, carried by an angel from heaven, spoke into his ear. "You have fought for three days, Dobrynya, fight for three more hours and you will have victory."

So the fight continued for another three hours, until Dobrynya found himself unhorsed and battling the dragon in a small crater on the mountainside. There, the dragon finally made a mistake. Rearing up in its anger, the dragon exposed its soft underbelly. Dobrynya took his chance and drove his Tartar spear deep into the unprotected flesh. The dragon cried out in pain, as Dobrynya ripped the spear free in a spray of blood. The dragon staggered and then collapsed, its weight falling upon Dobrynya and pinning him to the ground.

Dazed, Dobrynya looked about and saw that everything below his waist was pinned under the dragon. All around, the dragon's blood flowed from the monster's many wounds, filling the shallow crater. Over three more days, the blood came up to Dobrynya's ears. Bereft of strength after his long battle, he knew that he would soon drown in his enemy's blood. He laid back and prepared for his own death.

Then the angel's voice came to him again and said, "Do not give up Dobrynya. You have won a great battle. Drive your spear into the earth and go free."

In that moment, energy once again filled Dobrynya's limbs. With a prayer, he drove his spear down into the earth, allowing it to soak up the dragon's blood. With the spear firmly planted, he used it to pull himself free of the dragon's corpse. Covered in blood, he staggered up from the crater and saw the princess, Zabava, standing by the mouth of the dragon's cave, surrounded by numerous other captives that he had rescued.

Courteous knight that he was, Dobrynya checked upon the captives to make sure that they were well. Then he did one more thing. Removing his blood-soaked armor and clothes, Dobrynya bathed in the waters of the River Puchai one more time.

(Opposite) *Dobrynya Nikitich and Zmey Gorynych*. In most Russian tales, and indeed most Slavic folklore, dragons are multi-headed creatures. While Eastern Europe contains a wealth of dragonslayer stories, they are only slowly being made available in English.

Dobrynya Nikitich and Zmey Gorynych is one of the most popular Russian byliny, the traditional folk songs of medieval Slavic culture. Thanks to a major cultural conservation effort in the nineteenth and twentieth centuries, Russia has preserved a huge body of byliny, including over seventy versions of the Dobrynya and the dragon story. This story is only one of the many tales to include Dobrynya, who is considered one of the "big three" bogatyrs (knights-errant) of Russian folklore, the other two being Ilya Muromets and Alyosha Popovich.

While the stories of the bogatyrs mostly exist in the land of fairytale, there are some who argue that both Dobrynya and his confrontation with the dragon have a historical basis. Dobrynya was the name of the uncle of Vladimir I, who ruled as Grand Prince of Kiev from 980–1015. It was during this reign that much of the population is thought to have been Christianized, and this may have included a mass baptism in the Pochaina River. Thus, some argue that the story is a metaphor for the rise of Christianity against the pagan dragon, which also explains why the story contains a Greek pilgrim's hat and the voice of heaven. However, it is just as possible that these Christian elements were later additions to an older, pagan tale.

While Dobrynya remains relatively unknown in the west, he is still a popular hero in Russia, where he continues to serve as the subject of numerous artworks.

DRAGONSLAYERS FROM AROUND THE WORLD

For the most part, the study of the development of the dragonslayer narrative is a study of European myth, legend, and folklore. Of the hundreds of dragonslaying stories that exist today, the vast majority come from the Christian and folkloric traditions, which grew out of earlier European and middle eastern mythology. That said, there are exceptions, and, depending on how far one is willing to stretch the definition of "dragon," stories of gods and heroes fighting giant serpents or lizard-like monsters can be found in nearly every culture on earth.

It should be noted, however, that even tales from other parts of the world, which may seem like classic dragonslayer stories, have often in fact been colored by European thinking. It has often been the case that early folklorists and translators, when encountering a strange or rare foreign word that they know only to mean some variety of monster, have ended up using the word "dragon," or at least borrowing elements of the dragon to try and explain these foreign concepts. It is unlikely, for example, Native Americans or Japanese thought of dragons in anything like the same terms as Europeans.

That aside, no discussion of dragonslayers would be complete without at least a nod to these other great heroes, who battled their own variety of dragons in the far corners of the earth. Contained here is a quick summary of four such heroes, two Native Americans, one Japanese, and one Maori.

Manabozho and the Fiery Serpents

In 1839, Henry Schoolcraft released a two-volume book entitled *Algic Researches* which collected some of the myths and legends of Algonquian, Wiyot, and Yurok tribes of Native Americans. Included in these stories is the tale of Manabozho, a Native American dragonslayer.

According to Schoolcraft, Manabozho was something of a Native American Hercules. He was the great-grandson of the moon, possessed of great strength and cunning wit, and could wield magical powers, including the ability to shape-shift into numerous different animals.

Hiawatha slaying the Kenabeek from his canoe. (North Wind Pictures Archive / Alamy)

In one of Manabozho's numerous adventures, he is tracking down an evil wizard in his canoe, when he encounters a pair of serpents of "enormous length and a bright color," which blocked the way and "hissed fire." The serpents inform Manabozho that he cannot pass, so, falling back on trickery, the wily warrior points and shouts, "Look behind you!" When the serpents turn and look, Manabozho paddles his canoe past them. He then draws out his bow and shoots the confused serpents from behind, killing them.

While the name Manabozho is nearly forgotten today, his adventures formed the basis for much of the narrative in *The Song of Hiawatha*, the epic poem by Henry Wordsworth Longfellow. In this poem, it is Hiawatha who goes on a series of adventures, including battling the fiery serpents, which Longfellow described as follows:

> Soon he reached the fiery serpents,
> The Kenabeek, the great serpents,
> Lying huge upon the water,
> Sparkling, rippling in the water,
> Lying coiled across the passage,
> With their blazing crests uplifted,
> Breathing fiery fogs and vapors,
> So that none could pass beyond them.

Ouatoga and Piasa, the Dragon-Bird

In 1673, a French Jesuit priest named Father Jacques Marquette led an expedition into an unexplored region of the middle Mississippi. During his journey, he discovered a rock-painting of a creature that looked something like a scaled lion, with the face of a man, antlers like a deer, and a long serpent-like tail. Over the years, many explorers passed by the site and mentioned the image in their writings, but none offered any explanation for its existence. That changed in 1836 when Professor John Russell wrote an article about the creature. He named it Piasa, "the bird that devours men," and told a story that was supposed to have come from the folklore of the Illinois tribe of Native Americans.

According to Russell, the Piasa was a large, winged creature that lived in the cliffs. For many years it lived peaceably with men, carrying off deer and buffalo. Then one day, after a great battle, the Piasa flew down from its cliffs and began to eat the corpses of the dead. Finding it liked the taste of human flesh, it began to attack the local villagers, carrying off small children. When this had continued for many moons, Chief Ouatoga sought advice from the Great Spirit. After nearly a month of meditation, the chief came up with a plan. Using himself as bait, the chief lured the Piasa down from the cliffs. Then his warriors, who had been in hiding, sprang up and shot poisoned arrows at the creature's unprotected wings. The arrows tore through its wings and prevented the Piasa from flying away. The braves then rushed in and finished it off with tomahawks and knives.

In all likelihood, this story is completely the creation of John Russell. The name "Piasa" is taken from a local stream, and there is no indication that the word means anything like what John Russell says. In fact, it is not clear if the original creature even had wings, as Father Marquette doesn't mention them. They don't appear in anyone's description until a sketch in the 1820s labelled "dragon-bird."

Unfortunately, the original painting is long gone. At some point, either the Native Americans or the European settlers adopted the destructive custom of shooting at the painting with firearms, and eventually the whole rock face was destroyed by quarrying. There have been several modern attempts to bring back the Piasa, which have met with varying degrees of success. Today, a large version of the painting can be seen on a rock face near Alton, Illinois.

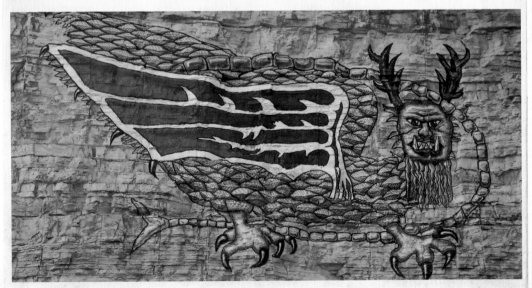

The Piasa as it appears in its current incarnation.

The word "Kenabeek" is Longfellow's version of the native word "genábik." Schoolcraft admits that this word is a generic one that can apply to "amphibious animals of large and venomous character," which is probably as close as most Native American languages came to having a word for dragon.

Pitaka and the Taniwha

According to the myths and legends of the Maori people of New Zealand, creatures called taniwha used to inhabit the waters in and around the island. The ocean variety of the monster looked like a giant shark of whale-like proportions, while the fresh water type more closely resembled giant lizards or dragons.

The role of these New Zealand dragons varied greatly in the different legends. In some stories, the taniwha served as loyal protectors of individuals, families or tribes. In others, they took the role of terrifying monsters that attacked from their watery lairs and dragged men down to their doom.

In one such tale, travelers on a road between two villages began to disappear. The men of one village, thinking the men of the other must be to blame, formed a war party and set off to attack their enemies. However, halfway to their destination, the warriors were attacked by a giant taniwha named Hotupuku. The dragon-lizard killed most of the men and sent the rest scampering back to their village. When the warriors related their story, a man named Pitaka came forward with a plan to kill Hotupuku. Taking a group of hunters and a great deal of rope, they went hunting for the dragon. When they got near its lair, they tied one end of their rope around a tree and made a noose out of the other end. Pitaka then went forward and lured the taniwha out. While Pitaka distracted it, the other hunters looped the noose around the dragon's tail, preventing it from escaping. Then they took another noose and managed to throw it around the dragon's neck. Lassoed from both ends, the dragon could only thrash about until it strangled itself on the rope. Pitaka then cut open the dragon's belly and found the remains of all the missing people, as well as weapons, jewelery, and sharks' teeth.

After this incident, Pitaka gained a reputation as a great dragonslayer, and sometime later, another tribe called on him for help. These people had been attacked by a taniwha named Pekehaua who lived in a large stream. Pitaka traveled to the village and observed the stream where the dragon lived. He then ordered the villagers to construct a large basket and fill it with rocks. When this was done, Pitaka and a few of his companions also got into the basket, and Pitaka ordered the basket be lowered into the stream. As the basket sank into the deep stream, Pitaka saw the dragon asleep at the stream bottom. Quietly, he swam out of the basket and slipped a noose around the dragon's neck. Then he tugged on the rope as a signal to the people back on land. The whole village was waiting there, and when they saw the signal, they all pulled upon the rope, pulling the dragon out of the stream onto land. The villagers then jumped upon the dragon, clubbing it to death.

Agatamori

Japanese dragons, like most Asian dragons, are usually gods or benign creatures and thus there are very few tales of Japanese dragonslayers. One notable exception is the legend of Agatamori, which supposedly occurred in the sixty-seventh year of the reign of Emperor Nintoku (around 379 CE). In that year, a mizuchi, a water-dragon, took up residence in a fork in the Kahashima River and began attacking passers-by with its poison breath.

An example of a Japanese style dragon.

As the death toll mounted, a local man named Agatamori set out to deal with the problem. When he reached the river, he waited for the dragon to emerge from its watery lair. When it did, he tossed three calabashes, a type of gourd, into the water. Agatamori then said to the dragon, "If you can sink these three calabashes, I will go away. If you cannot, I will take my sword and kill you."

The dragon agreed to this challenge and attempted to sink the calabashes, even turning into a deer at one point to try and push them under the water, but try as he might, the calabashes kept bobbing to the surface. As the dragon's failure became clear, Agatamori charged into the river and drew his sword, lopping off the dragon's head in one single motion. Then, to be sure that the river was clear, he dove down to the river bottom. There he found a whole family of mizuchi and slaughtered them all. So great was the killing that the river was stained red with dragons' blood, and forever afterward the spot in the river was known as Agatamori's Pool.

The story of Agatamori is found in the *Nihon Shoki*, "The Chronicles of Japan." Written in the Classical Chinese language around the year 720 CE, the *Nihon Shoki* is a collection of myths, legends, and early history of Japan. The inclusion of the Agatamori tale is really just a minor aside. The story falls into the classic folktale tradition of using an event, such as the slaying of a dragon, to explain a place name. It also doubles to give one family a heroic, dragonslaying ancestor, as Agatamori is stated to be an ancestor of the Kasa-no-omi clan.

Glossary

Adder: Snake.

Berserker: A Norse warrior known to fight in a frantic, frenzied manner.

Byliny: Folk song about legendary Russian heroes.

Cacophony: Harsh, dissonant sounds that do not blend.

Canonize: To officially declare someone a saint in the Roman Catholic Church.

Catapult: A mechanical device used to hurl or launch objects.

Celt: Ancient European peoples who lived in ancient England and other parts of western Europe.

Codify: To arrange laws or customs into a societal system.

Demi-god: The offspring of a god and a mortal.

Doctrine: A set of beliefs held by a particular group.

Ecumenical: Promoting Christian unity.

Epic: A long-form poem that tells the heroic adventures of a legendary person or place.

Hydra: A tubelike creature that lives in fresh water.

Knuckers: Water dragons.

Mizuchi: A water dragon.

Pestilential: Harmful to crops and livestock.

Rune: Letter in an ancient alphabet.

Secular: Describing something that does not relate to religion.

Visigoth: Western tribe of the Goths, a Germanic people who threatened the Roman Empire.

Wyrm: Dragon.

Wyvern: A two-legged dragon with wings.

For More Information

The Arizona Center for Medieval and Renaissance Studies
Arizona State University
P.O. Box 874402
Tempe, AZ 85287-4402
Website: http://www.acmrs.org
The Arizona Center for Medieval and Renaissance Studies (ACMRS) was
      founded in 1981 as a state-wide research unit charged with stimulating
      the interdisciplinary exploration of medieval and Renaissance culture.
      Its activities cover a period roughly from 400 to 1700 CE.

International Center of Medieval Art
The Cloisters
Fort Tryon Park
New York, NY 10040
(212) 928-1146
Website: http://www.medievalart.org/
The International Center of Medieval Art is a worldwide organization
      dedicated to the study of medieval art and culture.

The Mythopoeic Society
P.O. Box 6707
Altadena, CA 91003
Website: http://www.mythsoc.org
The Mythopoeic Society is an organization promoting the study, discussion,
      and enjoyment of fantastic and mythopoeic literature through books
      and periodicals, annual conferences, discussion groups, awards, and
      more. Its members are especially interested in the works of J.R.R.
      Tolkien, C.S. Lewis, and Charles Williams, prominent members
      of the informal Oxford literary circle known as the "Inklings"
      (1930s-1950s).

The Renaissance Society of America
CUNY Graduate Center
365 Fifth Avenue, Rm 5400
New York, NY 10016
(212) 817-2130
Website: http://www.rsa.org
Founded in 1954, the Renaissance Society of America promotes the study of
      the period 1300–1650. The RSA brings together scholars from many

backgrounds in a wide variety of disciplines from North America and around the world.

Science Fiction Research Association
P.O. Box 214441
Auburn Hills, MI 48321
Website: http://sfra.org
The Science Fiction Research Association (SFRA) is the oldest professional organization for the study of science fiction and fantasy literature and film. Founded in 1970, the SFRA was organized to improve classroom teaching; to encourage and assist scholarship; and to evaluate and publicize new books and magazines dealing with fantastic literature and film, teaching methods and materials, and allied media performances.

SF Canada
7433 East River Road
Washago, ON L0K 2B0
Canada
Website: http://northbynotwest.com/sfcanada-wp
SF Canada exists to foster a sense of community among Canadian writers of speculative fiction, to improve communication, to foster the growth of quality writing, to lobby on behalf of Canadian writers, and to encourage the translation of Canadian speculative fiction. SF Canada supports positive social action.

The Sunburst Award Society
2 Farm Greenway
Toronto, ON M3A 3M2
Canada
secretary@sunburstaward.org
Website: http://www.sunburstaward.org
The Sunburst Award for Excellence in Canadian Literature of the Fantastic is a juried award to recognize stellar writing in two categories: adult and young adult. The awards are presented annually to Canadian writers with a speculative fiction novel or book-length collection of speculative fiction published any time during the previous calendar year.

WEBSITES

Because of the changing nature of Internet links, Rosen Publishing has developed an online list of websites related to the subject of this book. This site is updated regularly. Please use this link to access this list:

http://www.rosenlinks.com/HERO/Drag

FOR FURTHER READING

Apollodorus. *The Library of Greek Mythology*, Robin Hard (trans.).
    Oxford, England: Oxford University Press, 2008.
Appollonius of Rhodes. *The Voyage of the Argo*, E. V. Rieu (trans.).
    London, England: Penguin Books, 1971.
Bailey, James and Ivanova, Tatyana. *An Anthology of Russian Folk Epics*.
    London, England: M. E. Sharpe, 1999.
Byock, Jesse L. (trans.). *The Saga of the Volsungs*. London, England: Penguin
    Books, 1999.
Edwards, Cyril (trans.). *The Nibelungenlied*. Oxford, England: Oxford
    University Press, 2010.
Evans, Johnathan. *Dragons: Myth & Legend*. London, England: Apple, 2008.
Grammaticus, Saxo. *The History of the Danes*. Books I – IX, Peter Fisher
    (trans.). Cambridge, England: D. S. Brewer, 2008.
Hargreaves, Joyce. *A Little History of Dragons*. Glastonbury, Scotland:
    Wooden Books. 2006.
Orbell, Margaret Rose. *A Concise Encyclopedia of Maori Myth and Legend*.
    Christchurch, New Zealand: Canterbury University Press, 1998.
Schoolcraft, Henry Rowe. *Algic Researches, Comprising Inquiries Respecting
    Mental Characteristics of the North American Indians*, Vol. 1.
    New York: Harper and Brothers, 1839.
Shuker, Karl. *Dragons: A Natural History*. New York: Simon & Schuster, 1995.
Siculus, Diodorus. *Library of History, Books II.35 – IV.58*, C. H. Oldfather
    (English trans.). Cambridge, MA: Harvard University Press, 2006.
Simpson, Jacqueline. *British Dragons*. London, England: B.T. Bratsford
    Ltd, 1980.

INDEX